"Porn, food, work, bad marr̲̲̲̲̲̲̲ someone who feels trapped. Maybe that someone is you. With over two decades of proven counseling experience, Andy Farmer takes his unique gift for 'simplifying-the-complex' and escorts the reader from the trappings of bondage to the soul-satisfying vistas of freedom. If you or someone you care about needs liberation, fresh hope and practical help await between these pages!"

Dave Harvey, Executive Director of Sojourn
Network; pastor of preaching at Four Oaks Church;
CCEF Board member; founder of AmICalled.com

"If you have ever been stuck, trapped, or cornered, then you know how hopeless it seems. You just do not know what to do. Andy Farmer wrote this book to help you experience the freedom found in a meaningful relationship with Jesus Christ. I encourage you to read it and let Andy lead you again and again to Jesus Christ."

Rob Green, Pastor of Counseling and Seminary
Ministries, Faith Church, Lafayette, IN

"*Trapped* speaks to a universal problem—feeling trapped in relationships, circumstances, and life. As Christians, we boast of the freedom that we have in the gospel and yet we still feel trapped. None of us are as free as we want to be, and many of us don't even understand what real freedom is. We live as if we must set ourselves free. Using five case studies of common traps, Andy Farmer carefully explains how to gain a freedom that we can't earn or win, a freedom that is a gift from God."

Jack Delk, Pastor for Counseling, North Campus
at Bethlehem Baptist Church, Minneapolis, MN

"Andy Farmer has written a very insightful, readable, and biblically-based book that applies the gospel of grace to those who have become ensnared or feel trapped in life. Its liberating truth provides a pathway to freedom, pointing to Christ as our Redeemer. As a pastor who longs to see people living transformed lives, I see this book as a great resource and one that I will want to recommend to others."

Ian Ashby, Lead Pastor, New Frontiers Church, Portsmouth, NH; Northeast Regional Leader, Newfrontiers USA

"Ever felt trapped and not known what to do? Andy Farmer's *Trapped* will help you get out of your trap and find true freedom in Christ."

Deepak Reju, Pastor of Biblical Counseling and Family Ministry, Capitol Hill Baptist Church, Washington, DC; author of *On Guard* and *The Pastor and Counseling*

"*Trapped* is a book about what so easily entangles us, but more so a reminder that we are free in Christ. It invites us to take another look at grace and the provision we have to live self-controlled, upright, and godly lives. If you have a bad habit, unhealthy relationship, or seemingly unsolvable problem, you need to read this book. Andy Farmer points us to the gospel afresh to break free from idols and to run to Christ and his redeeming grace. I recommend this for anyone who is trapped or those in the process of bearing with and restoring those who are."

Garrett Higbee, Executive Director, Biblical Soul Care at Harvest Bible Chapel; Executive Director, Biblical Counseling Coalition

"There is something about being human that craves freedom and loathes confinement. So we try to bust loose from something or someone, only to find that we still don't feel free. It is at this point—when we think that freedom might be an illusion—that Andy offers us a better way. Just read the first ten pages and he will engage you in this better way."

Edward T. Welch, CCEF Faculty; psychologist; best-selling author

"Here you will not find simplistic formulas. But if you really want to be free from the complex webs that entrap you, read this book. Andy Farmer's penetrating insight and wise guidance were learned through the struggle of escaping his own traps and decades of helping others escape theirs. He will lead you to the fundamental truth that will set you free."

Jon Bloom, Author and Cofounder of Desiring God

Trapped

Getting Free from People, Patterns, and Problems

ANDY FARMER

New
Growth
Press

WWW.NEWGROWTHPRESS.COM

New Growth Press, Greensboro, NC 27404
www.newgrowthpress.com

Cover Design: Faceout Books, faceoutstudio.com
Typesetting: Lisa Parnell, lparnell.com

ISBN: 978-1-942572-81-7 (Print)
ISBN: 978-1-942572-82-4 (eBook)

Library of Congress Cataloging-in-Publication Data
    Names: Farmer, Andy, 1959– author.
    Title: Trapped : getting free from people, patterns, and problems / Andy Farmer.
    Description: Greensboro, NC : New Growth Press, 2016.
    Identifiers: LCCN 2016009376 | ISBN 9781942572817 (trade paper)
    Subjects: LCSH: Liberty—Religious aspects—Christianity.
    Classification: LCC BT810.3 .F37 2016 | DDC 233/.7—dc23
    LC record available at https://lccn.loc.gov/2016009376

Printed in the United States of America

23 22 21 20 19 18 17 16   1 2 3 4 5

This book is dedicated to my wife Jill,
who shared the message of redemption
with me thirty-five years ago.
She has always been the greatest example
of a heart set free to serve the Lord
that I have ever encountered.

CONTENTS

ACKNOWLEDGMENTS

I'd like to thank the pastors and people of Covenant Fellowship Church and Risen Hope Church for living and sharing the redeeming love of Christ. You inspire me to take what I see in you and share it with others. That's what this book is about.

Thank you to Barb and Sue at New Growth Press for having a vision for this book and pushing me to make it the best it could be.

ACKNOWLEDGMENT

INTRODUCTION

When I was growing up, I had a fixation on the Frankenstein monster. It started by watching the old Boris Karloff films on the Saturday afternoon *Monster Movie Matinee* on our UHF channel. But I would feed the fixation by saving up my money to buy the monster magazines that were sold at the local five-and-ten-cent store. The magazines were filled with pictures of all my favorite movie monsters: not just Frankenstein, but Dracula, Wolfman, the Creature from the Black Lagoon, and others. But Big Frank was my favorite. I remember hours sitting at my desk, carefully copying the pictures in the magazine, trying to draw my favorite monster in exact and frightening detail.

One thing I loved as I lay awake at night was to plot escape plans out of my house if Frankenstein ever made it to my neighborhood. I imagined hearing him bursting through the front door while I was alone in my house. (Why he was after me was never something I considered. It's pointless to speculate on the motives of something that is only alive because of a huge electrical jolt.) In my scenario I had just enough time to run downstairs to the basement, taking advantage of the fact that the monster didn't know the layout of my house like I did. The other thing I was counting on is that Frankenstein wasn't all that fleet of foot with those big clunky shoes. I knew that if Wolfman was after me I was a dead man, but I had a shot to get away from Frankenstein if I had a good escape plan.

My best plan was to run out the basement door, jump the fence into my neighbor's yard, and then run down to the creek at the bottom of the hill. From there I would crawl through the drainage culvert under the street and emerge on the other side, safe under the cover of the woods. That's as far as my imagination could take me. The key to my whole plan was to never let myself get trapped where I didn't have a way of escape.

I think back on those idyllic days when all I had to worry about was being trapped by fake monsters. But as we grow, we begin to realize that there are plenty of real things around us that can feel like traps. Pressures and responsibilities in life. Health concerns. Family trials. Financial burdens. Fears of terrorism and crime. Aging, and caring for aging parents, can feel like a trap. Graduating from college and realizing that there are no good jobs in your field can feel like a trap. To feel trapped means we see no means of escape or release, and little hope for anything to change. One therapist writes that patients who feel trapped by something in life are overwhelmed by guilt, diminished self-worth, exhaustion, hopelessness, and depression. They feel frantic, scatterbrained, and inept. Another writer talks about people she's treated being "trapped in their seemingly never-ending cycle of chaos, crisis, or drama."[1]

I see these same struggles in people I meet with as a pastor. For the Bible-believing Christians who are my primary community, there is an added burden: they feel that they are failing God. Or God is failing them. They know that God has the power to set people free. They have read about it in the Bible; they may have even experienced a sense of freedom and victory over struggles at points. But life comes hard at you no matter what you believe. And it isn't surprising that we feel trapped when that happens. To feel that part of your trap is a God-problem just adds to the sense of despair.

At the heart of this book is a singular conviction: The promise of the gospel is not enduring captivity, it is enduring freedom. But this promise isn't plug and play. It doesn't just happen because you say you have faith. I do a lot of pastoral counseling and one of the most common struggles I see in those I counsel is how the gospel seems to get lost in the traps and trials they experience. Good, solid, believing Christians face hardships in life and have very little idea of how the gospel is meant to make a difference.

A few years ago I read a book by Jerry Bridges called *The Gospel for Real Life*. Bridges wrote it because he was concerned that the average Christian has what he calls a "truncated view of the gospel."[2] One thing he said really connected the dots for me.

> The reality of present-day Christendom is that most professing Christians actually know very little of the gospel, let alone understand its implications for their day-to-day lives. My perception is that most of them know just enough gospel to get inside the door of the kingdom. They know nothing of the unsearchable riches of Christ.[3]

I saw this very thing in so many people that I wanted to find resources to help people apply the gospel to their real-life problems. I function in a faith community where there is a renewed focus on the centrality of the gospel in every area of life. The amount of quality resources available on gospel-centered living is something for which I am enthusiastically grateful.

But I had a challenge finding books that took what Bridges calls "the riches of the gospel" (and what classical theologians call our inheritance in the gospel), and applied these great themes to specific, present-day, life-entrapping problems. So that's what I'm trying to do in this book. We live in a world full of traps and chains—sometimes of our own making, sometimes beyond our control. Many people feel trapped, and they look to God for freedom. So how is the gospel applied to trapped people? What achievement of the cross can a trapped person latch onto for hope and faith, so that the trap can be sprung and the chains broken? What is it about the gospel that sets us free? That's what I'm about in this book.

So how should you read it? Well, I hope you'll start at the beginning and work through to the end. That's why I wrote it the way I did. But I'm a realist. You have probably picked this book up because the title or table of contents speaks to something in your life. Maybe a particular trap resonates with you. If you see something like that, start there. If you find it helpful, then I invite you to read the first four chapters. They will help you take what you've read to a deeper level.

The gospel is glorious; it is the storyline of the Bible. The more you see your story in the story of the Bible, the more you'll see the bigness and goodness of God. And if you get that far in your reading, I'd love for you to read the rest of the book. Because I think trapped people can help other trapped people. Who knows, what you read here may help you be part of God's freedom project for others as well!

Chapter 1

REAL PEOPLE IN REAL TRAPS

I moved to the Philadelphia area back in the early 1980s. I've come to love the city for its rich culture and sometimes quirky history. Case in point. There is an old abandoned prison in Philadelphia called Eastern State Penitentiary. It's in an area that is now fairly gentrified—an eleven-acre fortress with thirty-foot brick and stone walls surrounded by an increasingly artsy neighborhood of townhouses, bistros, and coffee shops. The prison opened in 1829 and closed for good in 1971. Eastern Penitentiary is a place where notorious gangster Al Capone did prison time. His cell, with its accumulated creature comforts, still sits the way he left it in 1929.

The prison is historically significant for its design. It was built according to a new (at the time) corrections philosophy that recommended extended solitary confinement for inmates for the purpose of "personal reflection and reform." The belief was that extended isolation was the way to cultivate "penitence" (hence the term *penitentiary*). The prison architecture consists of seven two-story cellblocks emanating like spokes from a central processing building. Each cellblock floor has small, one-person cells along both sides of a single hallway. Its neo-gothic design added to its imposing emotional effect on prisoners. Today, the prison is a national historic landmark, but it is most popular for its "Terror Behind the Walls" Halloween haunted house.

TRAPPED IN THE PRISON OF LIFE

Imagine we are walking through a cellblock like the ones at Eastern State. On both sides are small dark rooms behind heavy wooden doors. Except this isn't a physical prison; it is a prison of human struggles. As we walk along the corridor, we see glimpses of prisoners through the small barred windows on the cell doors. In some cells we see prisoners busy at work at little desks, as if they don't even know they're behind bars. In other cells we see more troubling things—prisoners sobbing in misery, others pounding their fists against the walls in defiance of their situation. Some see us coming and run to the window, trying to get our attention, our sympathy, some human connection. Others just lie on their cots with faces turned to the wall.

We ask our guide, "Why are these people here?"

"Different reasons. Some, well, it almost seems like they wanted to come here. One bad decision after another and eventually this is where you end up. Others were just going through life and things happened, and they still don't know how they got here. Some have adjusted to it; it's almost like they would rather stay in the cell than get out. Others are fighting against it with everything they've got. But there's not much a fist can do against a prison wall. Most give up after a while. It's sad, but I guess that's what spending your life trapped in prison will do to you."

That's not a cheerful opening illustration, but it gets at why I'm writing this book. As a pastor and counselor, I spend a great deal of my ministry in the prison cells of human need. The people I meet with are often bound in things that practical advice won't solve. Usually they are getting by in life, but not always. The problems are diverse but the experience is fairly consistent. People come to me because they feel trapped in something and they can't get out. They feel caught in problems, behavior patterns, or relationships that control their lives. They use words like "stuck," "tied down," and "bound up" to express the way life feels. People feel weighed down by chains or shut in by walls or locked up in cages. And yes, they talk as if they are hopeless prisoners of their own lives.

I want to take you on a tour of this prison experience as I see it. We're going to pass cells in which people are trapped in a life-defining struggle. Some you'll be very familiar with, some you may not. There are far more jail cells of human trial than we'll have the time to visit, but I've chosen several because they are very common in our world today. Perhaps we know the despair of one of these cells from our own experience or the experience of someone close to us. Maybe you'll see yourself in one of these traps. Maybe your trap is different, but like the redundant sameness of cell after cell in a prison, you see the same things in your trap as you do in one here.

The good news is that we are not going to leave these prisoners in solitary confinement. The goal of this book is freedom.

When we leave this tour, we'll consider what makes a liberating difference for the prisons that trap us in life.

THE APPROVAL TRAP

The resident of the first cell we come to is Ellen. Ellen has been caught in the approval trap. She grew up in a high-achievement home. Academics had been her parents' identity; they wanted education to be valued by their kids. As the youngest child, Ellen had the additional burden of two older siblings who were following in the family footsteps of high grades and academic accomplishment. But Ellen wasn't wired that way. She was artistic, and that didn't translate to success in her parents' eyes. She longed for their approval but found it only came when she did something notable in school. As she entered her teens, she stopped caring about school. Ellen resented her family because she couldn't achieve in a way that mattered to them. She looked for a different "family" at school, a group that would accept her as she was.

She found it in the "fringe" kids, a diverse mix of teens whose commonality was that they all felt like failures at school and nobodies at home. For the first time, Ellen felt liberated from the standards of her family and free to be what she wanted to be. She began to change—to dress differently, listen to different music, hang out in different places. Conflicts with her parents became the norm and this only pushed her further into her new world of freedom.

But this freedom had a cost. Even the fringe had clear standards of behavior if you wanted to belong. It included drug use and, for the girls, it required participating in hook-ups and serial sexual relationships. Ellen did what it took to be accepted.

She dropped out of high school but then got her GED because her parents threatened to kick her out of the house if she didn't graduate. As her group got beyond the high school years, it began to fragment. By that time Ellen had fallen into a relationship with a guy she met at a party. "I knew he was kind of a loser, but he was there and it was better than being alone. Until he started drinking more and his anger came out. He had this instinct for manipulating my feelings. He'd use guilt and threats to keep me dependent on him. And if I ever started talking about leaving, he'd totally change his tune, telling me how much he loved me and couldn't live without me. That would just wrap me back under him again. Every time. Till he found a woman who made more money than me. Then he was gone without even saying goodbye."

That was eight years ago. You would hope that Ellen had learned her lesson on how to avoid losers. But she hasn't. Her life seems to bounce from one bad relationship to another. When she dates rockers, she becomes a groupie. When she dates an artist, she dabbles with painting. One time it was an intellectual. By the time that ended six months later, she had a library of books she'd never read and a philosophical vocabulary she'd never use again. Ellen is a thirty-year-old woman with a lifetime of experience and no identity to show for it. What she longs for is freedom to be who she is, beyond the expectations and demands of others.

THE LAZINESS TRAP

Drew is stuck in the laziness trap. He has always been a likable guy. In some ways he's the ideal friend. He's low maintenance, he's willing to go along with the group, and he never argues. What you don't want to do is depend on him for anything that needs to be done on time or in a certain way. Drew may eventually get around to it, but keep your expectations low.

Drew's a habitual procrastinator. He makes plans and even puts things in his calendar. But if it's up to him to get something done, it will inevitably be at the last minute, hastily thrown together in a stressed-out frenzy of activity. He says he works best under pressure, but those around him wouldn't agree. Because when Drew is under pressure, he is not very likable. Easygoing Drew becomes irritable Drew. He expects everybody around him to accommodate his rush and he gets angry when something doesn't go his way. If he doesn't get things done on time, it's never his fault. Something he didn't plan for (but should have) got in the way. Somebody else dropped the ball.

Procrastination and unfulfilled commitments have become such a common theme in his life that his friends don't even confront him on it. He may say he's sorry, but they never feel he understands how his lack of follow-through affects people. He just seems to move on. His friends employ the catch-all phrase, "That's just Drew—you've got to love him; you just wish you could count on him." When he's by himself, though, Drew does realize he's lazy. "I don't want to be like this. I always feel like a failure. My boss says I could really move up in my career if I just put the effort in, but I just do enough to get by. I've got all these ideas of things I want to do, but that's all they are—pipe dreams that will never happen. People think it doesn't bother me, but it does. But it's too hard to change. I joke a lot about being lazy, how great it is to be free from worry in life. But wasting your life isn't living. It's just getting used to being stuck."

THE EATING DISORDER TRAP

If it's six a.m., you know where to find Maria. She's at the gym religiously every morning, even on weekends. She's a treadmill beast. Other regulars at the gym ask her how she does it—how does she keep it up? She tells them she's in training. There's a 10K here, a bike race there—got to stay in shape! Except she's never entered a race in her life.

At work everybody likes to congregate around the office kitchen. It's a social time where employees talk about the news and vacations and whatever. Maria is typically there right around noon. If you see her, she's always smiling, always has a little banter for somebody at the microwave as she slips toward the fridge.

"Hey, Maria, we've got pizza from the meeting today. Come have some." "Thanks guys," she responds politely. "I love pizza, but I've got a race this weekend, so I just made myself some high protein stuff."

"Well, sit down with us. We're talking about our favorite shows." Maria glances at the empty seat at the break table and her little Tupperware container. "No thanks. I'm really backed up today. I'm just going to do a working lunch."

With a cordial laugh she leaves the kitchen and makes her way back into her office where she closes the door, opens her container, and dumps the contents into the trash. Every time.

From the moment she gets in her car at the end of the day, Maria has one thing on her mind. Double fudge chocolate cake. Today she doesn't have any more cake mix. She stops at the grocery store and buys five boxes, plus some extra cans of frosting. She gets home to her apartment, stops for a minute to feed the cat, and then retrieves her nighttime wear, a baggy warm-up suit from a drawer full of baggy warm-up suits. Just before putting it on, she steps on the digital scale. She doesn't like the number she sees. For the first time all day, her perpetually sunny expression is pierced by an angry scowl. She walks over to the full-length mirror to assess the damage. People tell her that she's too thin, but what she sees staring back at her is a repulsive hulk of misshapen fat and excess weight. She can't bear to see it, yet she can't bring herself to turn away. After a few moments she punches her leg hard, a common ritual that somehow frees her from her trance in front of the mirror.

In the kitchen she bakes in silence. She's made so many double fudge chocolate cakes that she could do it in her sleep. While it's baking, she surfs the net, always looking at fashion, at the thin but shapely models who seem to fill every outfit just right.

The cake is done. All that's needed is the spoon and the remote. Maria settles down in front of the flat screen with her only meal of the day. Within an hour she will have consumed an entire chocolate cake. Within an hour and a half she will have purged most of it in the bathroom. Within two hours she is in bed, trying to bury the nightly shame under a down comforter.

Tomorrow is another day. She'd like to be free of the self-loathing, but she knows what she'll see in the mirror tomorrow. And the mirror never lies. That's Maria's life. She is trapped by an eating disorder and thinks that this prison is where she belongs.

THE PORNOGRAPHY TRAP

Steven looked around the room at the other men in the circle. It was about as ordinary a gang of guys as he could imagine. Guys in jeans, in suits, with beards, with tattoos, with polo shirts, with baseball caps, with shaved heads. And here he was—yet again.

Charlie, the group leader, starts the meeting. "How are we doing? Anyone struggling this week?"

This is Steven's cue. He knows the drill.

"I really blew it last night. My wife took the kids to see her mom for the weekend. I told her where I'd be the whole time she was gone. Promised I'd just read and go to bed. I had the guys in my accountability group on alert, only a text away from me. But I guess that wasn't enough."

All eyes turn toward Steven. "What happened?" Charlie asks.

"I was sitting on my porch reading and I saw a woman walking her dog. She was pretty far away, but from a distance she reminded me of this girl I used to date. I started thinking about her and those times. Ask me now and I can tell you how bad that relationship really was. But right then all I could remember was how good it felt, no kids, no responsibilities, no disappointed wife. Just passion and breakups. I knew I was going down a bad road, but I couldn't help wondering, *Where is she now?* So I went on Facebook to look her up. Most of her info is private but I saw a couple of pictures. Not bad for twenty years later. But I thought, *That's it, I'm too close to the line.*"

"Then what?"

"You know those little ads on the sidebar in Facebook? For some reason I hadn't blocked access and one came up—you know what they are. I was on my phone so I couldn't see it much. But the girl in the picture, well, I couldn't resist. I clicked on it. Next thing I know, there's another link, then another. I was gone. It was like I was in my own little world—again. It must have been four hours by the time I got done."

Ken jumps into the conversation. "What about your rescue calls? Did you think to call somebody?"

"Sure I did. I thought, *I'm one click away from getting out of this.* But I couldn't do it. The pathetic thing is that I got two calls during that time. One was from my wife—I wasn't about to take that one. The other was from Tom, my accountability partner. I couldn't believe he'd call. I let it go. Then I told myself, *I've already screwed up big time. What's the point of turning back now?* So I just kept going. But it wasn't exciting anymore. It almost felt like, well, like I had to give in to it—that drive, you know what I mean.

"So here I am. More guilt. A wife who's disgusted with me and won't even leave me at home alone to go to the store. And all these images floating around in my head, coming at me in my sleep, at work, in church. And I've got to come in here and talk about it with all of you. It's humiliating. I'm trapped in porn and I don't even know if I want out anymore."

All the eyes in the circle turn toward the floor. It's an all-too-familiar story.

THE SUBSTANCE ABUSE TRAP

Dear Joan,

I hope you and all your family are doing well. I'm writing to let you know that Lorraine is back in rehab. We thought the last time had really done it. She came out and seemed so much like her old self. We were able to get her a job as a waitress at Bobby's restaurant. It wasn't much, but it's not like her track record with jobs was that good. She seemed to be excited to go to work and was bringing home some good tips. She enrolled again in community college, said she could go to school during the day and work nights. We were worried it might be too much right off the bat, but she was so positive we didn't want to dampen the enthusiasm.

That lasted for a couple of months. Then we started seeing the same old things we saw when she was using. We noticed she was sleeping in a lot after a night at work, missing classes. Of course we'd ask her if everything was okay and of course she would say it was great, just tired and stressed from school and work. She started smoking again; that's never a good sign. We really got worried when she'd start getting all these texts and calls on the weekends. She says they were friends from work. She'd never talk to anybody in front of us—she'd just get up and go into another room. Sometimes she'd come out and say it was somebody in trouble who needed to talk with her and she'd leave without telling us where she was going.

She started stealing from us. A couple of weeks ago I confronted her. I asked her if she was doing drugs again and if she had taken my money. She got really defensive and accused me of being paranoid and judging her. Usually I get intimidated but this time I stood up to her. I told her I didn't trust her, and that this is the kind of thing she does when she's abusing drugs. I told to her to prove it to me if she wasn't. She just cursed at me and rolled over and wouldn't talk anymore.

I thought we were heading down that awful road where you just don't know if you're going to get a call from the police saying your daughter is dead of an overdose. But fate intervened. She overslept a mandatory meeting with her probation officer and then, when they did a blood test, they found drugs in her system. I hate to see her back in trouble, but I feel like some time in jail and then rehab again is better than the hole she was digging for herself.

I remember one time you said you pray to God. I'm not a spiritual person but I'd appreciate if you'd pray for Lorraine. And if you think about it, pray for me as well.

Ann

TRAPPED IN A TROUBLED MARRIAGE

Michael:
I don't know what happened to her.

Tina:
I don't know what happened to him.

Michael:
Before we got married, she worked out and kept fit. I felt like, when we went out, people looked at her and she turned heads. It made me proud to be with her. Now

she doesn't seem to care what she looks like. No makeup, frumpy clothes, never does anything with her hair. It's like she doesn't care.

Tina:

Before we were married we'd go for long walks and just talk. I felt like I could tell him anything. Now he just comes home from work and turns on the tube. If he isn't watching sports, he's on his laptop or his phone. If I want to ask him a question, I feel like I need an appointment. I don't know the last time he actually looked me in the eyes. It's like he doesn't care.

Michael:

All she cares about is shopping. Every time I come home there's something new in the house. Some little knick-knack she got on the internet because she saw it on one of those home decoration shows she's always watching. Buying things is like a drug to her; she just can't get enough. When I try to get her to budget, she just laughs. All I am is an ATM in this marriage.

Tina:

All he cares about is work. He's out of the house before I get up, even though I know he doesn't need to be in till nine. I'm shocked if he gets home before seven. He expects dinner as soon as he gets home, which he eats in front of the tube. I can pretty much guarantee weekends are going to be about his job. We'll start a project and he'll get a call; then he's done for the day. All I am is a property manager in this marriage.

Michael:

And when she gets mad, oh man, that's out of hand! I know the neighbors think we're nuts. She'll say anything in an argument. And then won't even remember it later on. What really gets me is that she can be in the middle of screaming and get a call on her cell phone. She takes the call all sweet and nice and, as soon as she's done, she's at it again. It's like a war with her. And she always needs to win.

Tina:

I don't like to argue, but sometimes that's the only thing that gets through to him. He'll do something mean or cut me down and then, when I react, he just stands there with that look like I'm crazy, and just say "What?" I try to tell him what he did and he starts the debate. He starts firing off all these arguments like he's at work. He never, ever admits he's wrong. It's like a competition to him. And he always needs to win.

Michael and Tina:

I had always hoped that I'd marry somebody I could build my life with. How did we get here? I feel like I'm trapped and I don't know how to get out.

TRAPPED BETWEEN TWO WORLDS

William is one of those guys of whom it is said, "He was born with a silver spoon in his mouth." His family lives in a big house in the best part of the town. William comes from a line of movers and shakers. He grew up with all the trappings of privilege—private school, acceptance in society, the best advantages. But he also experienced some of the downside of being well-to-do. You wake up every day with the expectations of people you never even met focused on you. You can't be just good; you have to be the best. At everything.

William came from a family of church-goers who understood being religious primarily as a duty required of those with good social breeding. But something unexpected happened to William. He encountered some people who seemed to have an authentic faith that went beyond religion. They called themselves Christians. He came to see himself the same way. Religion stopped being a duty for William and started being a way of life.

After graduation from college, he moved as expected into the family business. But William the Christian constantly wrestled with how to live out his faith in a world that seemed to trivialize Christianity, if not dismiss it altogether. Today he continues to find himself between two worlds. Both call for his allegiance, his best time, his heart. He doesn't know how to navigate between the two—how to be successful in the one without compromising in the other. Every choice is a moral dilemma. Should I make this deal, should I go to that party? Can I be friends with these people?

Sometimes he struggles with guilt about how much he has and how much others lack. And he carries a deep burden for his family, who think he's nuts and hope this is just a religious phase. Would things be easier if he just tried to go into some type of ministry? At least he wouldn't feel so torn all the time. He hopes to make a difference in both worlds, but he more often feels like a failure and hypocrite. Does he love this world too much? Is he so heavenly-minded he's no earthly good? Sometimes he'd like to find an escape from the trap of living between this world and the world beyond.

WE NEED HELP TO GET FREE

The stories above are about real people, though I've changed details as necessary to keep them confidential. In some sense they are composites; in fact, I'm in more than one of the vignettes myself. My guess is that you are too. We're going to revisit each of these stories in the second half of the book. Metaphorically speaking, we'll go into each cell and look more closely at what it's like to be in these traps and how people get there.

You and I want out of traps, but we don't know how to get free. The good news is that, for every person caught in a trap, there is hope of freedom. There is life beyond the prison doors. And you can get there.

But first we need to consider the story of a man, a box, and a quest for freedom.

Chapter 2

NOT AS FREE
AS WE WANT TO BE

Dan, the whiskey-drinking delivery man, walked out the door at 107 N. Fifth Street, Philadelphia, a brick office building about two miles from Eastern Penitentiary. In his hand was enough money to treat himself to a good time at the local pub. It was considerably more than he'd expected for delivering a crate just a few blocks down the street. It was still morning, but a good day's work had already been done.

As the door locked behind him, four men in the office turned their gaze to the box he had left behind. They looked at each other with anxious anticipation, and then back at the box. One of them then did something that would have made Whiskey Dan think he really needed that drink. Rapping on the box with his fist, he spoke down to it.

"Is all right within?"

From within the box came a faint reply, "All right."

The four men then set excitedly upon the box, prying it open to reveal a man—a black man—soaked with sweat and semi-delirious. Rising unsteadily from the crate, the man stretched out his hand to his gawking liberators.

"How do you do, gentlemen?"

It was late March 1849. Two days earlier, Virginia slave Henry Brown, with the help of a couple of abolitionist sympathizers, had nailed himself into a two-feet long, three-feet wide and two-and-a-half-feet deep shipping box. The wooden crate was labeled "dry goods" and was addressed to the depot of the Adams Express Company in Philadelphia. At a stocky five foot eight inches and 200 pounds, Henry Brown squeezed himself into the crate with only a bladder of water and a few biscuits for nourishment. Then the lid was nailed shut.

The 250-mile journey from Richmond to Philadelphia would ultimately take him twenty-six hours, transported by wagon, railroad, steamboat, and ferry. At one point the box, which had been stenciled "This Side Up With Care" on its side, was carelessly tossed upside down, leaving the escaping slave stuck on his head for several hours. During one of many lulls in the journey, two transport workers began speculating on what might be in the box. Unnerved by the possibility that the workers would poke around the box and discover him, Henry was relieved when they decided that it must contain mail. The real male in the crate continued undetected along his appointed delivery route.

Had Henry Brown been discovered, he would have been treated as a fugitive slave, sent in shackles back to his owner, severely and publicly beaten, and perhaps even executed as an example to other slaves. And even if he hadn't been discovered, the journey itself could easily have killed him. Why would anyone trap himself in a wooden crate with only a crack in the joint for air and no certain hope he would ever get out?

One word. Freedom.

Henry "Box" Brown was trapped in the evil bondage of slavery. Nothing about him belonged to him. His possessions, his home, his body, his relationships, his talents, his choices all were owned by someone else. He had been born into slavery and knew no other existence. Though Henry saw freedom all around him in the way white people lived, he was under no illusion that he was anything but a slave. He knew what it meant to be treated and sold as property; he had seen what happened to those who didn't submit under the tyrannical thumb of institutional enslavement. Finally, as he watched his wife and children traded and carted off to a far-off plantation, something snapped in Henry Brown. There was nothing else slavery could take but his life, and he decided he would gamble that on the hope of freedom.

The atrocious institution of slavery is a deep stain on our national identity that can never be purged away. In its most profound human sense, Henry Brown's desperate choice to risk all for freedom is unfathomable to someone like me, who has only known the privilege of a free society. Yet in the world around us, people are going to unimaginable and often deadly lengths to escape war-torn countries, persecution, and grinding poverty. They stuff themselves into rotting boats, pick their way through borders lined with mines, and leave all their earthly possessions behind for the slim hope that freedom will meet them at the end. What is it about freedom that would invite such resolute abandon? How much would you risk for your freedom?

This may be an impossible question to ask in our Western culture. The United States was founded as a constitutionally free country. Embedded in our history is a resolve to "Live free or die," as the state motto of New Hampshire declares. In the rallying cry of Patrick Henry, "Give me liberty or give me death," our forefathers risked everything to declare their right to freedom through self-governance. That it took a tragic Civil War for that freedom to be legally extended to all Americans cannot be minimized. But this "freedom project" known as the United States continues to move forward in fits and starts even to the present.

So how free are we? At first glance, the answer is obvious. We are the free-est people in the history of civilization. As citizens we have more mobility, more ability to acquire the things we need and want, more access to information and knowledge, more civil liberties protecting what we say and do, more ability to make something of our lives, than anyone in any other era of history could imagine.

But it is also clear that not everyone in the U.S. has this experience of freedom. Gallup conducts an annual international poll[1] that tracks the perception of freedom in different countries. In response to the question, "In this country, are you satisfied or dissatisfied with your freedom to choose what you do with your life?" the July 2014 poll placed the United States at 36th out of 120 countries polled. The "Land of the Free" trailed progressive countries like Sweden and the Netherlands, and also trailed (by a significant distance) countries that would seem far more restrictive, like Cambodia, the United Arab Emirates, and Uzbekistan.

So maybe we're not as free as we wish we were. It's easy to find reasons for this dissatisfaction with our constitutionally guaranteed freedom: economic and social inequality, government inefficiency, partisan politics, rising distrust in traditional social and economic institutions, shrinking purchasing power. Ever since 9/11, we've been collectively debating how much freedom we're willing to give up for security. But there are more than socio-political factors in play in our sense of eroding freedom.

The pace of life itself can feel entrapping. You know the feeling. Why don't we wake up in the morning with boundless enthusiasm for the endless possibilities to exercise our freedom that stretch out in the day before us? Maybe it's because most of us, within the first few bleary-eyed moments of the day, are already receiving a list of "to do's" and "to be's" from our internal taskmaster. Before we've kicked off the bed covers, we've grabbed the smartphone, ingested all the new demands that came to us through email, texts, and social media, and taken up the burdens of the world through our news and Twitter feeds. To top off the fun, we pull up the calendar to take a gander at the impossible agenda we've set for ourselves today. Before we've washed the sleep out of our eyes, we are shackled to fresh chains of responsibility and demands that we will drag through another harried and distracted day. That's normal life, and it doesn't seem all that free. Yet we can't seem to break out of the busyness. As on-line writer Rachael Dymski has noted, "There is something deceitfully empowering about being busy. Americans have made it, at least in practice, one of our nation's crowning virtues—life, liberty, and the pursuit of perpetual busyness. We wear our busyness as The Great Burden, our mouths proclaiming we wish to be free of it, our hands grasping desperately to keep it within reach and on display."[2]

And then there are the life issues that spring-traps on us. The folks we met in the previous chapter are longing for some kind of freedom. They may not know exactly what that looks like, but they don't like where they are. They may feel hopeless, but if they could get a reboot on a different life operating system, it wouldn't be a bad thing. If you told them that twenty-four hours in a wooden box would get them out of their trap, most of them would probably take you up on it. The question is, what stands between our traps and our freedom?

WE DON'T UNDERSTAND OUR TRAPS

For some of us, the experience of being trapped in life is acute; words like chains, walls, prison, oppression, and even slavery are not inaccurate ways to describe what we deal with. We're going to address some of those in later chapters—life-dominating addictions, pervasive lusts, suffocating marriages—but these are just a few of the traps people live with every day. We can be trapped in financial ruin, in physical infirmity, in dead-end jobs, in the consequences of poor decisions, in victimization or neglect by others, in racial, ethnic, gender, or age boxes that others construct for us. But we may not understand our traps the way we should.

Sometimes we feel trapped but don't know what's keeping us there. Charles called me and said he had come to the end of the rope in his marriage. He had tried everything he knew to do, but his wife seemed to oppose any attempt he made to fix the problems in their marriage. He was trapped in a marriage with a woman who didn't want to be there but who seemed committed to making him as miserable as she was. He asked if I could meet with them and help her see how she was destroying their marriage. I agreed to meet, but I was pretty confident that there was more going on than Charles was reporting.

When we got together, I found a withdrawn woman who did little more than roll her eyes and harrumph as Charles made his case. At one point I took a moment to offer Charles what I thought was a gentle observation on his tone of voice when speaking to his wife. He went off on me, declaring in a loud and defiant way that he wasn't there to be attacked and that if I wasn't going to deal with her, there was no reason to waste time talking about nothing. I had a strong urge to roll my eyes and harrumph, but successfully fought down the temptation. It was very apparent that Charles felt trapped in his marriage, but he didn't realize that his hair-trigger temper responses and confidence in his own rightness might be part of the problem. He had helped build the very walls that he was accusing his wife of defending.

Here's another interesting thing about traps. You would think that if we felt trapped, we'd do anything to get free. You would think that Charles would be desperate enough to admit that what he was doing wasn't working and to ask about alternatives. But Charles is like many of us. We say we want to be free, but we don't want the personal regime change that freedom requires. We may subtly prefer a long-term life chained to our problems to the short-term hardship of doing what it takes to live another way.

Some people may not know they're trapped, or maybe they don't even care. This tends to happen when we find some benefit to the trap we're sitting in. We can adapt in remarkable ways to traps that give us something in return. We've already looked at the busyness trap. But there are others as well. Take career, for example. Career advancement seems like a good thing. It can offer so much of what we want—material things, the esteem of others, a sense of personal worth. But career success can be a trap that hides its costs to family, to a well-rounded life. Debt is another tricky trap. Credit card advertisements promise all kinds of freedom to have more and do more in life, but they hide the bondage of high interest payments. When we like some of the things we get in our traps, we often don't see the problem until we're in over our heads. Sadly, some people adapt to their traps so well that they don't care about the difference freedom could make in their lives.

It's likely you've read this far because you feel trapped in some way. You're hoping to find a way out. That's a good thing, because you can't get out of a trap if you don't know you're in one. Once you know you're trapped, you're ready to consider the solution.

WE DON'T KNOW WHAT IT MEANS TO BE FREE

Freedom is more than getting out of the traps that hold us. Ultimately, how we understand freedom will determine what we do about the things in life that keep us trapped.

Let's stop here so I can let you know that we're about to get philosophical. There's just no way around it. The question "What is freedom?" is a biggie in the world of philosophy. So the next few paragraphs are an important but hopefully painless attempt to get a sense of what we mean when we use what one philosopher called "the weasel word"[3] freedom.

Philosophers and theologians generally agree that freedom means the absence of constraints and limits to do and be what we want to do and be. In this sense, freedom can be understood as the opposite of slavery or tyranny. But there is also a positive aspect: people must actually possess what it takes to live in freedom. What good is it to be declared free if you lack the means to live the way you want? To philosophers, you can't be truly free if you don't have what it takes to exercise that freedom. But from this point on, it gets messy.

For example: How much freedom is possible? Is it possible to have total freedom, with no limits or inhibitions on what we can do and be? It may seem obvious that the answer to this question is no, but philosophers love to start with an ultimate idea and work back to experience. For example, if total freedom isn't possible, then what do we really want? Partial freedom? Occasional freedom? Is freedom real or is it just an illusion? Now you're getting into the very complex free will/determinism debate. In my research, I read entire books on this and couldn't tell you what I was supposed to get out of it. But the bottom line is that real freedom is not boundless freedom. There are limits on how much we can be free.

Let's add theology to the equation. If there is an all-controlling God somewhere out there, can I still be free? If there is a god (and philosophers love to talk about god if you can use the word "if"), does he/she/it limit my freedom? Can there be freedom in any way if there is a god who can and will meddle in human affairs? If God is over all things, then can there be any human freedom?

Do we have inalienable rights to freedom? Isn't this what the Declaration of Independence declares—the inalienable right to life, *liberty*, and the pursuit of happiness? What rights do we have to express our freedom? What if my pursuit of freedom infringes on your pursuit of freedom? What if what I want to do and be means I'm your master and you are my slave (or I am the despot and you are the common rabble who supports my rule)? Obviously we can't have an absolute right to freedom.

What do I do if I don't have freedom? Does society or government have the responsibility to make sure I have everything I think I need to pursue my freedom? If that fails, do I have a moral obligation to fight for freedom? To rebel against what I perceive as tyranny? Another question: Am I free to voluntarily give up my freedom? To exchange it for something like security that I might want more? We talk about freedom of speech, freedom to own guns, to worship, to marry who we want, to handle our bodies the way we want, to live without the intolerance of others. But all these "freedoms" are very controversial in our culture. As Will Rogers is famously quoted, freedom doesn't work as well in practice as it does in speeches.

Maybe we've soaked in the philosophical pool enough. But it gives you a sense of the complexity of what's involved when we talk about freedom. Let me try to bring it down to the world of pop culture. While I was doing research for this book, I put together a streaming playlist of songs about freedom. I've composed a little free verse poem from the lyrics that have bored into my brain over the past few months. Maybe this will help get a handle on the true meaning of freedom—at least what pop/rock/hip hop/country/reggae/folk/punk/metal tell me freedom means. It goes something like this:

It's a great day for freedom.
Freedom comes in a flash. It comes in a fight. It comes in a bottle.
It comes if we wait for it. It comes if we grab it when we can.
Freedom tastes like reality. It feels like a bluebird flying by me.
Freedom shouts from the mountaintops. It's an open sail on a distant shore. Freedom is marijuana trees blowing in the breeze.
Freedom is a road and a truck to drive on it. Or a drive on the freeway of love in a pink Cadillac. But if you're looking for the devil, he's out on Freedom's Road.

Freedom is a simple song the whole world should be singing.
It's just another word for nothing left to lose.
People got to be free. Find the cost of freedom.
Stand your ground and ring the bells of freedom.
Gaze upon the chimes of freedom flashing.
Watch the flags of freedom flying.

Did I tell you I just want to be free?
Your love will free me. But if you love somebody you've got to set them free.
I've got to break free from love.
I'm free as a bird now, and this bird you cannot change.
No right, no wrong, no rules for me, I'm free.

I'm free and easy. I'm wild and free. I'm running
free. I'm free-falling.
I won't stop till I find my freedom.
I wish I knew how it feels to be free.

REAL FREEDOM FOR REAL TRAPS

"I wish I knew how it feels to be free." This is an idea that
resonates with all of us, because all of us at some point find ourselves trapped in life. In the first chapter we looked at people in
serious need of freedom. They aren't in a literal prison. They're
not unusual people. They are people you might coach soccer
against or do playgroup with. People who work in the cubicle
next to you or brew the coffee you stop for every morning. But
they feel trapped in something or by something and they can't
get out. My guess is that you will know one of them in some
way. Maybe you'll be one of them. It's for these people that I'm
writing this book, and hopefully for you as well.

One thing these stories have in common is this: People stay
in traps because they can't free themselves on their own. As
much as we might long to escape from whatever traps we find
ourselves in, we likely need something beyond ourselves to liberate us. Traps don't open by themselves; chains don't fall off
unless they are unlocked; walls don't tumble down without a
force to topple them. We'll see as we go along that each of the
people in chapter 1 needs something to intervene to set them
on the road of freedom. If you feel trapped in life, you probably
also know deep down that you can't get free without help from
something or someone beyond yourself.

The sense that we are trapped by various circumstances, limits, and weaknesses in life is a reality every human being experiences. This deeper bondage doesn't sit well with us because we weren't made to live it. I think our desire for freedom means we were, in fact, designed for freedom. And so we yearn for it, strive for it, maybe even idolize it. And one day, somehow, we hope to have it.

But do we truly know what it feels like to be free? The freedom we were designed for may be unfamiliar to us. It is a freedom we don't earn and can't win. I contend that it is a gift from the God who has made us with the capacity for real freedom. I hope to give you a vision of freedom that doesn't get bogged down in philosophy or truncated by the limits in life that we all experience. I want to stir up a desire for that freedom and help you see how a life of true freedom—full, deep, and joyous freedom—is possible, here and now, in a world full of traps, cages, chains, and walls.

Chapter 3

THE BIG TRAP AND THE GREAT REDEMPTION

About five blocks south of Eastern State Penitentiary is the focal point of one of the great art debates in Philadelphia history. The controversy centered on the question, "Is this art?" The focus of attention was a statue prominently positioned at the entrance to the city's world-class Museum of Art. Philly was divided. Proponents of the statue thought that it perfectly captured the spirit of the city. Opponents couldn't believe that right-minded people would even consider the hulking bronze figure "art."

The statue was known simply as "Rocky." It was (and is) an eight-and-a-half-foot tall depiction of Rocky Balboa, the fictional up-from-the-streets boxer from the seemingly endless motion picture franchise created, produced, directed by, and starring Sylvester Stallone. The statue was actually a prop, a depiction of Rocky (Stallone) in triumphal pose that had been featured in *Rocky III* (and later in a cameo in *Rocky V*). In the movies, the statue was located at the top of a long stone staircase that Rocky climbed at the completion of iconic training montages in several of the films. The steps also happen to be the majestic front entrance to the Art Museum, one of the city's great cultural institutions. Hence the controversy.

In a sense, there shouldn't have been a controversy. No one really claims Rocky is a work of art—it's a movie prop! A pop celebrity actor captured in bronze. But the museum faced intense public pressure from city tourism interests, who saw the statue as a great draw for out-of-towners. And they were dealing with ordinary Philadelphians who had come to see themselves in Rocky, and saw in his story something of what they wanted to see in their own.

REDEMPTION STORIES

Sylvester Stallone tapped into a universal theme with Rocky. It is why city and art museum officials finally compromised and gave Rocky his own place of honor near (but not on) the Art Museum steps. It is why people from all over the world flock to the museum with the goal of seeing Rocky and "running the Rocky Steps." Rocky is a kind of modern redemption story. "Just another bum from the neighborhood" (as Rocky says) trapped in lower-class poverty and ignorance is given one shot at a way out through an undeserved title fight. Rocky seizes that opportunity, makes the best of it, finds love, and achieves a kind of freedom to finally do and be what he wants to do and be. It's no accident that the climactic fight with Apollo Creed takes place in the Cradle of Liberty on Independence Day.

We love redemption stories. We want to be reminded that the traps that ensnare us, the chains that bind us, the burdens that weigh us down, the walls that hem us in, won't keep us down forever. Somewhere out there something is going to intervene and deliver us—give us a way to freedom that we can't find on our own. What makes a story redemptive is not just the predicament of the person who is trapped, but the risk or cost to the person who steps in to bring deliverance. Redemption isn't just a powerful hero coming to the rescue; it requires something of the deliverer. The champ, Apollo Creed, offers Rocky redemption through an undeserved shot at a title fight. This costly redemption is depicted in greater depth in Victor Hugo's *Les Misérables*, as main characters Fantine, Eponine, and Jean Valjean all sacrifice their lives for the freedom of Marius and Cosette. J. R. R. Tolkien filled his Hobbit and Ring stories with characters who took great risks and paid terrible costs for the sake of main characters. More recently, the Harry Potter stories culminate with a small body count of beloved characters who give their lives to deliver Harry and his friends from the evil Lord Voldemort. From Baloo the Bear in *The Jungle Book* to Anna in *Frozen*, Disney has built a modern animation canon around redemption stories.

The people we met in chapter 1 need redemption. They are trapped. For some, the trap is largely of their own making. For others, it seems like cruel fate has overtaken them and, as much as they struggle to get free, nothing will change. Do you see yourself in one of those traps? Maybe your prison cell isn't one we have visited, but you know what it means to be trapped. You're longing for a freedom you can't get on your own.

This book exists because there is a redemption story that can really set you free. Not just inspire you, not just help you get by or adapt to hopeless circumstances. This redemption story is vividly real and endlessly relevant. Simply put, it exists to make you free. To explore it, we need to leave Philadelphia and travel across the world and back in time to ancient Palestine. It is there we will encounter the One who is known as the Redeemer, Jesus of Nazareth. We will meet him walking along the dusty roads outside Jerusalem. He is about launch into a teaching moment. You don't want to miss it.

BEWARE THE TEACHING MOMENT

Have you ever been the focus of a teaching moment? Teaching moments happen when people who don't know better do or say something that reveals just how much they don't know. Then everybody gets to learn from their example.

Here's an example. I played youth football growing up. Toward the end of a long practice, the coach wanted us to do one more drill. From out of nowhere some kid said, "But coach, we're tired!" I thought to myself, *Who is the dumb kid whining about football practice?* As I looked around, I noticed everybody looking at me. It suddenly occurred to me that I was the dumb kid.

If you know anything about football practice, you know that complaining invites the teaching moment. Grabbing me by the shoulder pads, the coach dragged me in front of the team. "Number 26 here says we're all tired. I think he wants us to all learn what it's like to be really tired. On the line. It's wind sprint time." Thus the entire team got a teaching moment on why you don't complain at football practice. For me, this teaching moment confirmed that I didn't want to play football all that bad. So I played soccer (where, incidentally, complaining and whining are totally okay).

No one practiced the art of the teaching moment better than Jesus of Nazareth. One of his greatest teaching moments occurs in Mark 10:32–45. It's a street scene—Jesus and his disciples on the Jericho Road, heading to Jerusalem for the Passover celebration. There is a sense of foreboding about this trip. Jesus's words and actions have created a confrontation with the powers-that-be. And they are headed straight to the center of the troubles. Jesus stops to contextualize the situation for them.

> "See, we are going up to Jerusalem, and the Son of Man will be delivered over to the chief priests and the scribes, and they will condemn him to death and deliver him over to the Gentiles. And they will mock him and spit on him, and flog him and kill him. And after three days he will rise." (Mark 10:33–34)

This is not a rallying cry. It is hard, frightening truth. You'd think that the effect would be sobering. Apparently not, because two of his closest friends, the brothers James and John, volunteer the situational cluelessness needed for a good teaching moment. James and John totally disregard the ominous words Jesus has just spoken and make what one commentary fittingly calls "an underhanded grab for greatness,"[1] asking Jesus to appoint them to sit in places of honor at his right and left hands when he comes into his kingdom (10:37). In short order Jesus seizes the moment and resets the agenda. The teaching moment isn't simply to expose the preposterous nature of their request. Jesus uses it to define the true nature of greatness (10:42–44). But then he takes the instruction far deeper.

> "For even the Son of Man came not to be served but to serve, and to give his life as a ransom for many." (Mark 10:45)

This brief sentence from Jesus will be our teaching moment in the pages ahead.

OF RANSOM AND REDEMPTION

The first thing you notice in this statement is that Jesus breaks into a third-person self-reference. This isn't some sort of celebrity narcissism trip. Jesus is using some powerful Old Testament imagery to alert his hearers to the fact that what he is saying is of cosmic and eternal significance. As biblical scholar Robert Peterson has noted, Jesus's self-designation as Son of Man combines "the mortal, insignificant 'son of man' of Psalm 8:4 . . . and the exalted, divine 'Son of man' of Daniel's prophecy (see Daniel 7:13–14)."[2] Peterson goes on to highlight Jesus's use of a past tense verb—the Son of Man *came*—as a declaration of his pre-existence. In other words, within a half sentence Jesus has affirmed his deity, described his essence, and set the stage for revealing his ultimate purpose. And what is that purpose? "To give his life as a ransom for many."

The word translated *ransom* is carefully chosen by Jesus to proclaim the theological significance of the coming death he has just described to them on the road. It's an economic term that was culturally understood in a very specific way. We have different terms in English to describe different types of financial exchanges. We can pay a fine, make a loan, buy a car, deposit a check, or charge a fee. *Ransom* was the term used when the financial transaction was paying the price to free a slave. When you used the word *ransom* in Jesus's day, people assumed you were talking about slave trade. The only way to "be" a ransom was to literally offer yourself as a payment to secure the freedom of someone who was a slave.

Do you understand what Jesus is saying? When he said he would be delivered over to the authorities, condemned, punished, and ultimately killed, he wasn't giving them a worst-case scenario. He wasn't revealing his intent to be a martyr for the cause. This horrible outcome wouldn't happen because the opposition was just too stubborn to convince or too strong to overcome. Jesus would not die like this because the plan was going to fail. This *is* the plan. Jesus came to die, and his death is the ransom, the payment, the cost of setting people free. "Many" people, he says. That includes you and me.

What's more, Jesus isn't just pointing ahead to what he will do. He is revealing why he will do it. His choice of the word *ransom* establishes the link between what he has come to do and what was done for the people of Israel in the exodus from Egypt centuries before. To understand what Jesus is saying here, we need to look at what happened there.

EXODUS: A REDEMPTION STORY FOR THE AGES

They had come to the land of Egypt as a small nomadic tribe; the Bible says there were no more than seventy among them (Exodus 1:5). We learn from the book of Genesis that they came to Egypt to escape a famine that ravaged the entire Fertile Crescent. Through the providence of their God Jehovah, one of them, who had been cast out years before, had gone on to ascend to a place of power in Egypt. The family followed him to Egypt with the approval of a pharaoh who appreciated the managerial foresight of Joseph the Israelite.

As the years went by, the small Israelite clan was fruitful and they multiplied throughout Egypt. Racial prejudice and fears of the growing numbers of this immigrant people gripped the Egyptians. Ignoring four hundred years of peaceful coexistence and the pivotal role Joseph had played in their survival, new rulers began to treat these non-Egyptians with contempt, as enemies of the state. Ultimately, the Israelites were forced into slavery. There was no earthly escape from bondage. But in the second chapter of the second book of the Bible, the stage is set for the great redemption we call the exodus.

> During those many days the king of Egypt died, and the people of Israel groaned because of their slavery and cried out for help. Their cry for rescue from slavery came up to God. And God heard their groaning, and God remembered his covenant with Abraham, with Isaac, and with Jacob. God saw the people of Israel—and God knew. (Exodus 2:23–25)

The Israelite people were trapped in slavery, spending every breath in servitude and oppression. They had seen hardship in their history, but they had never before been a people in bondage. So they cried out. They lifted their despair in pleas to the God who had always been there for their forefathers—Jehovah Jireh, the God who provides (Genesis 22:14). The passage above uses four verbs to describe God's response to their cries: he heard, he remembered, he saw, and he knew. These words in the original Hebrew convey something like this: God heard their groaning with the ears of mercy and compassion, and he was indignant about the injustice of their bondage. Nothing escaped his gaze. Acting out of his faithfulness to the covenant promises he had made to their patriarch Abraham, God set about the work of deliverance.

Immediately following this, the Exodus account gathers momentum. First, God calls Moses as his chosen servant at the burning bush (3:1–12) and commissions and empowers him to go to Pharaoh to demand the release of the Israelites from slavery (3:13—4:17). Moses returns to Egypt (4:18–31) for his first disastrous confrontation with Pharaoh (5:1–21), and falls into despair over his failure—"Why did you ever send me?" (5:22).

In response to Moses's plea to be released from his appointed role, God gives him a glimpse of the larger eternal history being written. In Exodus 6 we peer into the deep counsel of God and discover the redemption that was a foreshadowing of what Jesus came to do centuries later.

God spoke to Moses and said to him, "I am the LORD. . . . I have heard the groaning of the people of Israel whom the Egyptians hold as slaves, and I have remembered my covenant. Say therefore to the people of Israel, 'I am the LORD, and I will bring you out from under the burdens of the Egyptians, and I will deliver you from slavery to them, and I will redeem you with an outstretched arm and with great acts of judgment. I will take you to be my people, and I will be your God, and you shall know that I am the LORD your God, who has brought you out from under the burdens of the Egyptians." (Exodus 6:2–7)

God describes to Moses what he will do: he will bring them out, he will deliver them, and he will redeem them. The first two phrases are somewhat synonymous but are meant to describe what will happen. God will not leave them in Egypt; he'll put distance between them and the conditions of their slavery by his own divine action. He is not going to foment a rebellion or revolution. He isn't unfolding an elaborate escape plan where all the Israelites suddenly make a mad dash for the border. They will be led out by the hand of God in full view of their oppressors.

The third phrase is the key. God says he will "redeem" his people. He doesn't have to use this word to describe the exodus, but the fact that he uses it has cosmic and eternal significance.

The Hebrew word group translated as *redeem* or *redeemer* is freighted with meaning. It is concerned with something being restored and preserved by someone who has the means to do so. The value of the redeemed thing is determined by the price the redeemer is willing to pay for it. From this same word group comes the term Jesus uses with the disciples—*ransom*.

To redeem someone is to buy him out of bondage. The price of that redemption is the ransom that is paid.

What Jehovah is saying in Exodus 6:6 is that he will "pay the cost" to set Israel free. You can draw a straight line from Exodus 6:6 ("I will redeem you with an outstretched arm") to Jesus's declaration to his followers in Mark 10. Jesus is telling his disciples that God's redeeming purposes for all humanity will soon be accomplished—through him. Jesus has come precisely for this purpose. He is about to be the ransom that will redeem those who are enslaved. All of the Old Testament, and Exodus in particular, points to the great eternal redemption that will be accomplished by Jesus. This astounding truth will be seen by the writers of the New Testament as an essential picture of the gospel itself, so much so that future generations will understand the message and work of Jesus Christ simply as "the plan of redemption."

REDEMPTION FROM THE GREAT TRAP

Jesus is telling the disciples that they are like the Jews in Egypt—oppressed and powerless slaves who can't free themselves. And we are trapped as well. With the same heart of Jehovah in the exodus story, Jesus's compassion goes out to the trapped and enslaved. He acts on behalf of those in bondage because of his mercy, not our merit. We need the freedom only he can purchase for us. To paraphrase Exodus 2:25, Jesus saw the many, and he knew. As he tells the disciples, he did not come to be served, but to serve. He is the promised Servant of God who came to "bring out the prisoners from the dungeon, from the prison those who sit in darkness" (Isaiah 42:7), "to proclaim liberty to the captives, and the opening of the prison to those who are bound" (Isaiah 61:1; Luke 4:18). We all need freedom. We all need Jesus.

In Exodus the trap is obvious: national slavery is the condition that moves God's heart to act. But what about us, the "many" that Jesus came to ransom? What are the chains and traps that enslave us? Jesus and the New Testament writers make it abundantly clear that we are enslaved by sin, so the ransom is paid to free us from sin. This is the slavery that binds all humanity, the eternal trap from which there is no human escape. Only Jesus can free people trapped in sin. Consider his words in an intense confrontation with his enemies in John 8.

> "I told you that you would die in your sins, for unless you believe that I am he you will die in your sins. . . . Truly, truly, I say to you, everyone who practices sin is a slave to sin. The slave does not remain in the house forever; the son remains forever. So if the Son sets you free, you will be free indeed." (John 8:24, 34–36)

We need to understand this idea of sin. Ask a dozen people to define the word *sin* and you will probably get a dozen answers. The concept of sin refers to the bad things that happen in the world God has made for good. Some people live feeling as if everything they do is sin; some live with the sense that everything other people do is sin. To some, sin is a moral word for the things people do that we generally regard as wrong. Murder is sin, lying is sin. But not everyone defines morality in the same way. For some, embellishing a story or holding back important facts from someone is the sin of lying; for others, it's not. For some, abortion is the sin of murder; for others, it is the legal termination of a pregnancy. In our complex world, there isn't as much moral clarity as we might wish. So what sin is and isn't can be a pretty divisive issue.

The Bible presents sin as a rejection of God's ways and the consequences of that choice. When the Bible tells us that we are redeemed from slavery to sin, it is talking about a universal human experience of being inescapably trapped by sin and its consequences. We see the blueprint for the trap of sin in the account of the fall in Genesis 3. Here we see the initial human impulse toward God-defying independence. Our forebears Adam and Eve turn away from the good and moral order that God designed for his creatures. Enticed by just enough outside temptation to stir foolish rebellion, they strike out in pursuit of a freedom and enjoyment of life beyond the Creator's dominion. They consciously and deliberately disregard and disobey the moral command of God in favor of their own ways.

But this rebellion has a horrible cost. There is no life independent of God; we were not created with that capacity. And God does not yield his moral right to rule to those who are not God. It is his divine will that orders and shapes the created universe, and no created being is above it or beyond it. So the serpentine tempter is cursed (though he remains an active enslaver in this world). Guilt and judgment fall upon Adam and Eve and all who follow them. With the curse come the inescapable consequences of life outside God's favor—spiritual darkness, brokenness and shame, cravings and lusts that rule our actions and choices, lives pocked with conflict and depravity, cultures and societies that enslave, oppress, and exploit. And in the end there is death—eternal punishment and separation from God. Sin is the trap and there is no way out.

How can anyone be set free from the trap of sin? Let's get back on the road with Jesus. Where is he heading? To Jerusalem? For what reason? Jesus and his disciples are going to Jerusalem to celebrate the Passover. The Passover—the spreading of blood over the doorways of a house to avert the angel of death—is *the* symbolic event that ties the Jewish people to their redemption from slavery in Exodus (Exodus 12). It is no coincidence that Jesus is on his way to Jerusalem for the Passover when he reveals the deeper meaning of his plan of redemption. He has come to die—to be the Passover Lamb.

All four Gospel writers usher us into the upper room in Jerusalem where Jesus celebrates his final Passover meal with his disciples. With this meal they are commemorating the redemption of God's people from slavery in Egypt. And it is here, in this moment, that Jesus most clearly declares why he has come. In accordance with Passover custom, Jesus holds up a cup of wine, the third cup in the ceremony, the cup called "the cup of salvation, the cup of blessing."[3] Mark quotes him as saying, "This is my blood of the covenant, which is poured out for many" (Mark 14:24). There it is again, "the many." The many to be ransomed will be ransomed by his blood.

Mark very intentionally threads this blood ransom message through his Passion account. We saw how Jesus confronted James and John about their ambitions with the question, "Are you able to drink the cup that I drink?" (Mark 10:38). It is this cup that Jesus alludes to in the upper room. And it is this cup that Jesus asks God to take from him in the Garden of Gethsemane. "Abba, Father, all things are possible for you. Remove this cup from me. Yet not what I will, but what you will" (Mark

14:36). We know from the rest of the story that on the cross, Jesus did drink the cup all the way down.

In theological terms this is known as the substitutionary atonement of Christ. It is the essence of the gospel and the key to freedom. In simple language, it means that Jesus accepted the punishment for sin that we deserved. He paid the price that was beyond our ability to pay. Jesus is the only human being (and the Bible makes it clear that he is fully human) who entered this world free of the bondage of sin, and he lived his life unfettered from the sins that ensnare you and me. He was the only truly free person who ever existed. Because he is one of us but free of sin, he could offer himself as the ransom, the substitutionary atonement, for the many. Because he is fully God, his precious blood is the full ransom price for the many. His payment is entirely sufficient to set free the many enslaved in sin. Nowhere is this substitutionary atonement for our redemption expressed with greater clarity and force than in the apostle Paul's words in Romans:

> For all have sinned and fall short of the glory of God, and are justified by his grace as a gift, through the redemption that is in Christ Jesus, whom God put forward as a propitiation by his blood, to be received by faith. This was to show God's righteousness, because in his divine forbearance he had passed over former sins. (Romans 3:23–25)

This passage reaches back to that awful night in Exodus 12 when God brought death upon all households who had not wiped the blood of a spotless lamb on their doorpost. Read the Passion narratives of any of the Gospels. As you do, remind yourself that this individual who is falsely accused, mocked, rejected by his own people, abandoned by his friends, railroaded to condemnation by mob rule, beaten to a pulp, degraded, humiliated, and finally put to death as the worst kind of criminal, is the eternal and glorious Son of God. Ask yourself, "Could God do more than this to free us from our sin? Could a greater ransom price be paid?" No! Our sin required it and his blood has secured it.

ARE YOU AMONG THE MANY?

Anyone can be among the many. If you describe yourself as a Christian, how did you get that way? We are not redeemed because we decide to believe in Jesus, or because we self-identify with the Christian religious tradition. We're not redeemed because we go to a Christian church, because we live a Christian lifestyle, because we made a "profession of faith," or because we have made ourselves acceptable to God. We are Christians because a merciful Redeemer paid the ransom for our redemption. There is nothing in us that makes us more redeemable than anyone else. All are trapped and all need to be redeemed. If you and I by faith believe that Jesus drank the cup of God's wrath intended for us, and died the death we deserved on our behalf, we are numbered among the redeemed.

The many is not the all. Jesus adds an important caveat to this promise of redemption. Not everyone is granted a place at Jesus's side. This is important for his immediate interaction with the disciples, because not all of them will be counted among the many. One will reject his need for the blood ransom and choose blood money instead (Mark 14:10–11, 43–44; see

also Matthew 27:6). We are never told in Scripture what ultimately motivated the disciple Judas to betray Jesus. We are just
left with the fact that one who knew Jesus intimately and heard
the gospel repeatedly in the end rejected it completely. Because
there is a Judas, we know that the many is not the all.

You and I must face the Judas test. As you have read this
chapter, you have been given all you need to know to see your
need for the Redeemer. To be counted among the many, you
must be convinced that you are trapped in sin and unable to
free yourself. To be counted among the many, you must believe
that Jesus is who he says he is, the Redeeming Savior whose
blood is the only ransom payment that can free you from the
bondage of sin. And you must forsake any other hope for freedom in this life or the next. I can't put it any better than the
great Princeton theologian Benjamin B. Warfield, who once
said:

> The real thing for you to settle in your minds, there-
> fore, is whether Christ is truly a Redeemer to you, and
> whether you find an actual Redeemer in Him—or are
> you ready to deny the Master that bought you, and to
> count His blood an unholy thing? Do you realize that
> Christ is your Ransomer and has actually shed His blood
> for you as your ransom? Do you realize that your salva-
> tion has been bought, bought at a tremendous price, at
> the price of nothing less than blood, and that the blood
> of Christ, the Holy One of God? Or, go a step further: do
> you realize that this Christ who has thus shed His blood
> for you is Himself your God?[4]

Chapter 4

REAL FREEDOM

In the last chapter we saw Jesus use a teaching moment to reveal his great redemptive purpose. What created the opportunity for a teaching moment with James and John was Jesus's description of his upcoming death (Mark 10:33–24). Jesus showed the disciples and us that this death would be the ransom that would redeem a world trapped in bondage to sin. But his prediction of what was about to happen in Jerusalem doesn't end with his atoning death on the cross. He ends with these words: "And after three days he will rise" (Mark 10:34).

The resurrection of Jesus is the cosmic game-changer. In coming out of the grave, Jesus broke our chains of slavery to sin and defeated the punishment of death. It is because of the resurrection that we have victory in Christ over the slavery to sin. In 1 Corinthians the apostle Paul stands on the resurrection side of Calvary and glories in the victory of Christ. Of first importance in Paul's celebration are the death of Christ for our sins and the resurrection (15:3–4). If Christ has not been raised, then we are still trapped in the curse of sin (15:17). But Jesus has been raised (15:20)! And he reigns over all (15:25). Therefore Paul can exult,

> "O death, where is your victory?
> O death, where is your sting?"
> The sting of death is sin, and the power of sin is the law. But thanks be to God, who gives us the victory through our Lord Jesus Christ. (1 Corinthians 15:55–57)

In upcoming chapters we will apply this victory to difficult life situations. But for now, consider this brief summary of the traps that no longer hold those who are free in Christ.

- Redemption is freedom from the curse of the Law (Galatians 3:13).
- Redemption is freedom from slavery to sin (John 8:34; Romans 6:17).
- Redemption is freedom from the sentence of death (Romans 7:4–6; 8:2).
- Redemption is freedom from the guilt of our trespasses and sins (Ephesians 1:7; Colossians 1:14).
- Redemption is freedom from the oppression of Satan (Matthew 12:22–29; Hebrews 2:15).
- Redemption is freedom from the deceptive snares of the world (2 Peter 2:18–21).

Truly, if the Son sets you free, you will be free indeed (John 8:36)!

REDEMPTION IS A HOLY FREEDOM

Let's take one more trip into Philadelphia. Less than half a block from where Henry Brown emerged from his box into freedom stands Independence Hall. In the sweltering summer of 1776, inside this stately brick colonial building, a group of lawyers and businessmen hammered out the principles and language that would form the Declaration of Independence. That document was read in public for the first time on July 4, 1776, from the steps of Independence Hall. Eleven years later, the leaders of thirteen now-independent colonies gathered again at the same building, during another sweltering Philadelphia summer, to hammer out a new Constitution. It was a contentious convention; Ben Franklin described the Constitutional Convention as "groping around in the dark." It seemed that the unity over independence from English rule that had been proclaimed so eloquently and forcefully in the Declaration had dissolved into confusion and disagreement on what an enduring freedom should be. In chapter 2, we talked about the problematic issue of freedom. The history of the United States is the journey of defining, defending, and struggling to apply this elusive vision of freedom that is so foundational to our national identity.

We know this experience on our spiritual journey as well. Lasting freedom can seem like an elusive thing. What happens when the chains come off, when the prison doors swing open? When the tyrant of sin is overthrown? Where do free people belong? Are we left to "grope around in the dark" or to run back into the familiar prisons we've made for ourselves? The question of what freedom should be is crucial if we're going to live in the good bought by the ransom of Christ.

Here is the key idea. The Bible gives us the wonderful news that we weren't simply redeemed *from* sin, we were redeemed *for* God! We have been brought out of sin into the gracious and loving reign of our Redeemer King.

This is so important for us to understand. We often talk about what it means to be a Christian, what it means to be "saved." One of the most important things it means is that we have been ransomed from the bondage of sin into the ownership of God. To be free means we belong to God! And those who belong to God are called to live for his glory.

This is beautifully proclaimed in the Exodus 6 covenant we read in the last chapter. "I will take you to be my people, and I will be your God" (Exodus 6:7) now includes all who by faith live in the victory of Christ. This promise is not deserved or earned; it is all by grace. But this is also a sanctifying covenant. God is our God, but we are also his people. We are owned by God. We belong entirely to him. Paul says it so clearly: "You are not your own, for you were bought with a price" (1 Corinthians 6:19–20).

Do you think like that? It's not natural to us! To be owned by God means that we live to do what he desires for us to do. We see ourselves as entirely dependent on him for life. It means that what he says is what we trust. Whenever we are tempted to live for ourselves, our own glory, or our own desires or preferences, we will turn away from those motivations toward obedience to Christ. It means that what he brings about in our lives is ultimately what we want to happen in our lives. It's radical, but this is the heartbeat of true freedom.

Anyone who seeks to live out this holy freedom in Christ will realize that it is not a natural fit. True holy freedom isn't something we're prone to seek. We need to unlearn the ways of life we learned in bondage to sin in order to embrace the freedom we've been given. In a sense, we are liberated people who need a "new constitution" to guide us in freedom. There are three key aspects of this constitutional freedom that we need to embrace.

EMBRACE THE GRACE IN YOUR FREEDOM

The first aspect we need to address is our tendency to live as if we can redeem ourselves. We all have our "redemption systems" that give us the sense that freedom is something we earn, deserve, or achieve. If you look closely enough, you'll see that each person we met in chapter 1 has his or her own redemption system. It may involve submitting to the standards of others (like Ellen, Maria, or William), or running from standards that seem too hard to fulfill (like Drew, Steven, or Lorraine), or exempting ourselves from standards because others fail to live up to our standards for them (like Michael and Tina). The common thread in all our man-made redemption systems is that *we* determine what standards apply to us. If we look closely at our lives, we will see this tendency. We have a schizophrenic relationship with moral and spiritual standards. We run to them to try to earn our standing with God and then we run away from them when we fail to reach that standard. This is the problem of legalism.

What is legalism? We sometimes equate legalism with religious actions, as in "I am spiritual, not legalistic." But legalism isn't just the performance of stale religious duty. It is any attempt to bring our good works (or lack of bad works) into the work of redemption. It is saying that we can help free ourselves from the trap of sin. This is self-righteousness—denying the gift of unmerited, ransoming grace that is essential to our redemption and freedom. Legalism will not embrace the grace of redemption.

One of the primary reasons that the apostle Paul wrote his letter to the Galatian church was to address the problem of legalism. The Galatians were Gentiles who had received the gospel and were seeking to live lives of faith in Jesus Christ. But some teachers of Jewish law had come into their midst and were calling people to "double convert"—to convert to Christ and then to convert to Judaism. To these teachers, the only way to live in holy freedom was to live the Jewish way. Paul, the converted Jew, would have none of it (Galatians 1:6–9; 3:1)! He spends the first four chapters of his letter in passionate and uncompromising appeal for them to reject this heresy as a war against "the grace of Christ" (Galatians 1:6). In Paul's words, they were seeking to be "justified by works of the law" (Galatians 2:16). Note that these Galatians weren't being required to deny Jesus—that would be persecution. They were being required to add just a little of their own initiative to the work Jesus had done to complete the redemption transaction. Galatians is the strongest argument in Scripture against legalism.

Throughout his broad-ranging theological argument, Paul uses the redemption language we have been exploring.

> Christ redeemed us from the curse of the law by becoming a curse for us . . . In the same way we also, when we were children, were enslaved to the elementary principles of the world. But when the fullness of time had come, God sent forth his Son, born of woman, born under the

law, to redeem those who were under the law . . . For freedom Christ has set us free; stand firm therefore, and do not submit again to a yoke of slavery. (Galatians 3:13; 4:3–5; 5:1)

What are your legalistic tendencies? Everyone has them. Where are you prone to perform for your freedom? Old habits die hard, and the habit of trying to justify ourselves before God is one of the oldest and hardest habits to kill. To kill self-justification Paul calls us to "stand firm" in our freedom—not work for it, but embrace the free grace in it. Puritan pastor Samuel Bolton issued a simple but powerful call to grace in the face of legalism.

Maintain your liberty in Christ by refusing to look any more to the law for justification, and by refusing to fear its words of condemnation. You are to live, in respect of your practice and obedience, as men who can neither be condemned by the law nor justified by it.[1]

EMBRACE THE IDENTITY IN YOUR FREEDOM

In the late 1960s lead singer Jim Morrison of the Doors gave voice to the modern impulse to see freedom as personal autonomy. "I'm interested in anything about revolt, disorder, chaos, especially activity that appears to have no meaning. It seems to me to be the road toward freedom."[2] Anarchist Adam Kokesh gives this radical independence a political spin: "Self-ownership is an integral part of being human. You own yourself. You own your body. You own your labor. For anyone to assert otherwise is to attempt to restrict your freedom or make you a slave."[3]

According to the Bible, however, this independence impulse is not a sign of freedom. There is no Independence Hall in the history of the redeemed. The demand for independence says far more about the problem of our bondage than its cure. We were never created to live as independent beings. We were created to be dependent on our Creator God for life, meaning, and identity. The bondage of sin has unleashed an independent streak in us that may seem initially like freedom. But we're not wired that way. Left to ourselves, we don't like independence. We will seek out something or someone to give us a sense of identity or meaning. And whoever or whatever that is will become our new trap.

What has come with our new freedom in Christ is not just liberty from sin but a new identity as well. The apostle Peter describes our identity this way:

> But you are a chosen race, a royal priesthood, a holy nation, a people for his own possession, that you may proclaim the excellencies of him who called you out of darkness into his marvelous light. Once you were not a people, but now you are God's people; once you had not received mercy, but now you have received mercy. Beloved, I urge you as sojourners and exiles to abstain from the passions of the flesh, which wage war against your soul. Keep your conduct among the Gentiles honorable, so that when they speak against you as evildoers, they may see your good deeds and glorify God on the day of visitation. (1 Peter 2:9–12)

Peter's words are meant to give us great security. They are drawn from the book of Exodus where God specifies what "I will be your God and you will be my people" will actually look like through the giving of the law (Exodus 19:2–6). Standing in the full reality of the resurrection victory of Jesus, Peter describes the identity of God's redeemed people in Christ. First, notice the definitive tense in Peter's words: You *are* a chosen race . . . you *are* God's people . . . you *have* received mercy. Jesus has paid the ransom and we are now God's possession. Those who belong to God will never be sold back into slavery to sin. Our freedom is an absolutely secure freedom. But, as Peter goes on to show, our experience of it is still partial. We are sojourners and exiles; we have not yet reached our land of freedom. But we are definitely on the right journey.

Also, notice the plural language. We are not on this journey alone. We have been redeemed *into* a people. This is so important in our day. We live in a world that sees the spiritual journey in overwhelmingly individualistic terms. It's my faith, my spirituality, my religion. It's much easier to exercise independence if we don't have to account for anyone but ourselves. But the Israelites on their pilgrimage would have had a hard time thinking of their sojourn as a personal quest. They lived in conscious awareness that they were part of a gathered people, and it framed the way they understood God's activity in their lives. Individual spirituality is inherently small, fragile, and prone to falter in the face of adversity. True freedom is never simply mine and mine alone.

The people we met in chapter 1 struggle with a sense of who they are and with what life is supposed to offer them. Something has hijacked their sense of identity. It may be the expectations or failures of others. The comforts of the world. The indulgence of the flesh. Bitterness and resentment. Addiction.

Destructive habits. At one time they looked at life in terms of its possibilities and adventures. Now they see only its trials and regrets. And, in a very personal way, they look at life alone.

However, if we are in Christ, we have been joined to his holy people, his church, and there is great security knowing that we are part of his great work of redemption in this world. Living with a sense of our collective freedom won't shield us from the hard things in life, but it will help us to better understand God's purposes in them. We are linked to God's redemptive work throughout history. Our journey has depth and meaning because it is part of the larger story of God's holy people, and we live out that identity before a world in desperate need of what we've been given.

You and I are little redemption stories on display to the people around us. As Peter says, a powerful motivation to resist sin and live godly lives is the desire for our redemption story to be compelling to others who need to be set free from their own bondage. We have a purpose. A world enslaved by the tyranny of sin looks on. As we embrace our identity together as God's people, others are meant to see something about our redemption and the Savior who has redeemed us.

EMBRACE THE CALLING IN YOUR FREEDOM

In 2000, the *USA Today* list of the year's 100 most fascinating personalities included a horse. His name was Zippy Chippy and his claim to fame was that he had raced eighty-six times and never won. By the time he finished his career in 2004, he had lost 100 races. What made Zippy Chippy fascinating was not the number of losses, but the way he lost. Zippy Chippy was a horse with the talent to win. But for whatever reason, he wouldn't try to win unless it was on his own terms. As his trainer once said, "He wants to see the other horses out in front of him before he runs. Then he tries to catch up to them. He once lost a race by sixty-seven lengths. But even when he loses, he comes back to the barn like a winner, kicking up his legs and prancing and twirling around with his tail up."

Zippy Chippy became a legend in racing circles. Whenever he raced, thousands of dollars would be wagered all over the country by racing enthusiasts who thought that this might be the time when he'd actually do what he was supposed to do. Eventually, some tracks refused to allow him to run because they considered it consumer fraud. It was left to his trainer to sum up the mindset of Zippy Chippy, the headstrong horse. "If this horse wanna run, he run. He give you the best he got. But he don't wanna run all the time. He's temperamental. Not everybody can be a winner. He's a horse that has personality. He does what he wants to do."[4]

Zippy Chippy's problem is not one of identity. He knows he's a racehorse. The problem is "he does what he wants to do." All of the people in chapter 1 struggle with this as well. If you asked any of them what they should do to resolve their problems, they could probably give you good answers.

"I need to make my own decisions," says Ellen.

"I need to stop procrastinating," says Drew.

"I need to work with a nutritionist," says Maria.

"I need better accountability," says Steven.

"I need rehab," says Lorraine.

"We need to communicate," say Michael and Tina.

"I need the right priorities," says William.

All good insights. Why don't they work? Because insight apart from application is just insight. And application doesn't happen without a larger vision of why we want to change. Counselors will tell you that if counselees just want to fix problems, they will have a difficult time making progress. But if they have a compelling vision of what they want to be or become, the chances that they will make hard choices and work through serious change is much higher. In other words, real change must start from the inside out.

Freedom in Christ is not just a new status. There is an inner work that begins when we are ransomed by Christ. It is deep work in the soul that begins the moment we receive Christ, and it continues throughout our lives. How does this happen? Paul declares that this work of inner freedom is the work of the Holy Spirit.

> Now the Lord is the Spirit, and where the Spirit of the Lord is, there is freedom. And we all, with unveiled face, beholding the glory of the Lord, are being transformed into the same image from one degree of glory to another. For this comes from the Lord who is the Spirit. (2 Corinthians 3:17–18)

The "we all" in verse 18 is another way of saying "the many" (see Mark 10:45). All who are set free in the Lord are being transformed into free people from the inside out. Freedom is radical transformation, begun at conversion but carried through from one degree of glory to another until we live the full body-and-soul freedom that has been secured for us in Christ.

How do we know if we are experiencing this new freedom? What do transformed people look like? Consider Jesus's followers after the resurrection. These are the same disciples who pushed for first place on the way to Jerusalem, the same disciples who deserted Jesus at the moment of his greatest need. But after the resurrection, their hearts are captured by the desire to live as servants of God. Nearly every New Testament letter begins with the writer introducing himself as "a servant" of Jesus Christ. The Greek word used is *doulos*, the word for bond-slave in New Testament times. While some commentators have sought to soften this to simply mean "worker," the reality is that a *doulos* was completely owned by someone else—in other words, a slave. In a society that saw autonomy as a high value, to be a slave, or to identify oneself as a slave, was to be known as something the world thought little of.

In his book *Slave of Christ*, biblical scholar Murray Harris thoroughly explores the idea that redemption brings a believer into a life of bond-service to the Lord (*Kyrios*) Jesus Christ. Harris discusses how people who witnessed the degradation of human slavery all around them would be willing to identify themselves that way—and even be treated that way by others.

> . . . while for Christian leaders *doulos* was already a title of honour, it gained its positive connotations in the ears of all Christians because the divine Master they were serving was kind and generous and himself had blazed an exemplary trail of lowly service. What all the *douloi* of this *Kyrios* gained through being associated with him was not so much authority and power as unparalleled honour and the assurance that their service, whatever its nature, was of supreme value, simply because it was done for *him*.[5]

Only someone experiencing the heart-changing power of grace can freely embrace the calling to live as an obedient servant of Christ. We know that God is at work in our lives, setting us free from our old allegiance to sin, when we experience a growing desire to find true joy as servants of our Lord and Redeemer Jesus Christ.

ON THE WAY TO FREEDOM

Do you struggle to enjoy the freedom for which you have been set free? You're not alone. We are all on that journey together. Sometimes the freedom road is tough traveling. Jesus never said it would be a smooth highway. But just because it is a hard road doesn't mean it isn't a glorious journey. The ultimate destination is full, complete, and eternal freedom in Christ. One theologian said it well: "Redemption is so great and vast that its full potential cannot be realized here and now. For that we must await the coming kingdom."[6]

Freedom for the people of God was purchased by the ransom blood of Christ and was secured by his resurrection. We enjoy that freedom here, but it reaches its fulfillment in the age to come. We see this promise of redemption fully realized in the book of Revelation.

> And they sang a new song, saying,
>   "Worthy are you to take the scroll
>   and to open its seals,
>   for you were slain, and by your blood you ransomed
>   people for God
>   from every tribe and language and people and nation,

and you have made them a kingdom and priests to
our God,
and they shall reign on the earth." (Revelation 5:9–10)

In the age to come, the Redeemer Lamb will be worshipped
by those who have been ransomed for God. No tribe or language or people or nation will be excluded. And all will be
kingdom priests, joyful servants, to our God.

That, my friends, is true freedom!

We're going to turn our attention to the way this true
freedom works for us now in the traps and chains of this life.
We're going to learn what really traps people in their quest for
approval and comfort, in unhealthy patterns of escape, in addictions, in toxic marriages, and in the demands of the culture
around them. But we won't stop there. We'll see how the gospel
of redemption brings clear and compelling freedom. We'll see
how the truth of God's Word provides both vision and practical wisdom for change. We'll see what sets people free from
traps and keeps them on the glorious road of redemption.

But before we do, please take time to reflect on what we've
considered in the last two chapters. You see, not everyone who
is trapped in slavery to sin is looking for freedom. Many are
rather comfortable in their traps, having accommodated themselves to the chains that hold them. But all this means is that
they don't understand the eternally perilous situation they are
in. Please don't be that person! There is no freedom apart from
Jesus Christ.

But for those who have been redeemed from the trap of sin
by the ransom blood of Christ, there is a joyous freedom that
will never end. As another Puritan pastor proclaimed,

Those who owed God more than they could pay by their eternal sufferings; those that were under the dreadful condemnation of the law, in the power of Satan, the strong man armed; those that were bound with so many chains in their spiritual prison—their understanding bound with ignorance, their wills with obstinacy, their hearts with impenetrable hardness, their affections with a thousand bewitching vanities, and who slighted their state of slavery so much as industriously to oppose all means of deliverance—for such persons to be set at liberty is the wonder of wonders, and will be marvelous in the eyes of believers forever.[7]

Chapter 5

THE APPROVAL TRAP

In chapter 1 we met Ellen. Ellen is caught in the approval trap. Her life has been built almost entirely around the expectations of others. She begins each day with somebody's face, voice, or opinion filling her world. Ask Ellen what she wants in life or what's most important to her, and she'll tell you about somebody else. What matters to the "somebody elses" in her world is what most matters to Ellen.

The approval trap is a tricky trap. It is built out of things that are very much part of who we are. We're social beings, which means that we navigate life in relationships. Think about how much your daily experience involves responding to the demands, needs, actions, attitudes, and roles of others around you. We naturally read people and respond to the signals they're sending to help us figure out our place in the world. Behavioral researchers are focusing on "mirror neurons" in the brain, which seem to engage when we observe or encounter the behaviors of others. Mirror neurons are the physiological triggers of our relational impulses. Relational impulses attune us to the social cues around us. Healthy relational impulses allow us to "play nicely" with others—to get along, to make friends, to show empathy, to tolerate differences, to know our proper place in the group.

But what happens if those relational impulses start to drive how we live in unhealthy ways? What happens if our sense of self is determined by our perceptions of what others think of us, or where we fit in some social group? What happens if, like Ellen, we allow people to so define who we are and how we think, feel, and act that the stock value of our life rises and falls on the wants, needs, or demands of someone else? It is then that we're caught in the approval trap.

Another thing that makes the approval trap tricky is that all of us live in it a little bit. In adolescence the approval trap is known as peer pressure. While peer pressure can have its dark side, it is usually considered a normal and manageable part of growing up. As we get older, the approval trap is known as "people pleasing," not something we relish being known for, but you can be called worse things. But there are darker expressions as well. Codependency, the compulsive need to be valued by someone else, was a trendy take on the approval trap a few years ago. Something that is getting a lot of attention these days is the notion of social phobia or social anxiety disorder. This tends to be a more obvious, life-controlling trap, where people develop distinct physical aversions to various types of social and relational interactions.

Once inside the approval trap, we are hooked to the perceived demands of others and an insatiable craving for their acceptance. We are simultaneously dependent on what people think of us and fearful of their evaluation. What someone actually thinks of us is often irrelevant—our perceptions matter most. So we learn to perform outwardly in ways that help us feel approved or at least avoid feelings of rejection.

It took a particularly traumatic failure of a romantic relationship for Ellen to take stock of the dysfunction and relational chaos of her life. With the help of counseling over time she was able to see how her craving for approval had controlled her life.

> For years I've hid behind walls constructed to protect my image and keep my life pain-free. Basically, I *lied!* I would tell only enough of what was going on in my life to keep from being totally exposed by everything coming apart. I had to handle things myself, I had to do it, I didn't need help, I could figure it out and make it work—I've been playing (and paying for) the "keep up appearances at all costs" game my entire life, trained to it since childhood. I've never told others the entire truth about my situations. How would that make me look? What would they think or do? They'd never understand. I'd be rejected again. . . . With impending disasters everywhere, I fell apart, but only when no one was looking. Ever the consummate actress, when people were around it was "Lights, camera, action." I was able to be whatever I needed to be to fit in.

It's not hard for me to identify with Ellen. Growing up, I was caught in the approval trap and didn't even know it. My clearest memories of elementary school involve constant comparisons. Whether it was comparing lunch boxes or craving to fit in on the playground, I was always measuring myself against whoever seemed most popular or cool in school. By the time I made it to high school, I had developed a conscious strategy for getting and keeping the approval of others. It was a three-point plan: (1) Don't make enemies, (2) Don't stand out, and (3) Don't be seen with the wrong people. I really lived this way. I wanted to be liked, to be able to walk into any social group or situation and feel like I fit in. I built my own approval trap with an incessant campaign for social acceptance.

What about you? What does your approval trap look like? Is it a conscious scheme to carve out a place of acceptance like mine? Is it a willingness to mold yourself to fit the perceived demands of others? Is it a tendency to overvalue the approval or affections of one person? Do you crave popularity? Do you dread rejection? Do the opinions of others rule your life? Do you live in fear that you won't measure up to some standard of behavior or appearance or "cool" in the world around you? Would you love to be free of the approval trap? There is a way.

THE FEAR OF MAN IS A SNARE

The Bible does us a huge favor in the way it describes the approval trap. The Scriptures call it the "fear of man." Why is this helpful? By defining the approval trap as the fear of man, we can begin to dismantle it from the inside out. A great place to start is with the simple words of Proverbs 29:25:

> The fear of man lays a snare,
> but whoever trusts in the LORD is safe.

This short verse gives us the key to freedom from the approval trap. We can either fear man or trust in the Lord. Counselor Ed Welch lays out the reality of this choice well.

All experiences of the fear of man share at least one common feature: people are big. They have grown to idolatrous proportions in our lives. They control us. Since there is no room in our hearts to worship both God and people, whenever people are big, God is not.[1]

People have always been big in Ellen's life. Her parents were hugely influential, setting the standard for her security and significance from early childhood. The fact that her siblings could meet these standards only intensified Ellen's feelings of failure when she couldn't measure up. She found a group where she felt accepted, but the group culture swallowed her up and she became indistinguishable from it. When the group fragmented, she was again alone, so she sought identity and acceptance in what she thought was romantic love. But it too was a snare, and her heart was broken time and again by men who got what they needed from her and then moved on.

Ellen had grown up without an understanding of God, so she only knew the "bigness" of people. She read lots of books on self-image. "What I kept reading was how I needed to be assertive. I needed to set boundaries in relationships and love myself most of all. But I feel like all I do then is live on constant high alert against toxic people. When you spend all your energy guarding yourself, it gets tired and old. And lonely."

Protecting ourselves from others doesn't set us free from the fear of man. The approval trap can't be sprung by managing the "people influences" around us. According to Proverbs, the answer doesn't lie in managing our relationships, but in change in our hearts. Safety from the snare of the fear of man requires "trust in the Lord." The fear of man takes hold when we take what belongs to God—our abiding trust, devotion, and willingness to have our lives shaped around his will for us—and place it on others. When we worship people, we require them to be something they can't be—absolutely trustworthy, good, and infallible. No one can meet that standard or carry that burden. Inevitably, even well-meaning people will disappoint us because we've made them into little gods. And little gods fall short of what we require them to do for us.

Where does a trust in the Lord come from? It comes through faith, through believing that Jesus sets us free from the false worship of others so that we can enter into the true worship of God. The answer for Ellen is not in self-protection and self-love. It is in allowing Jesus to liberate her from the fear of man and bring her into the safety of God's ownership and eternal approval. Ellen needs this freedom, and so do we.

STEERING CLEAR OF THE SNARE

We have a great example of this in the New Testament. Perhaps no one in the Bible stumbled in and out of the snare of the fear of man more than Peter the disciple. Throughout Jesus's earthly ministry, Peter emerged as a natural leader. Jesus himself singled Peter out as an example of the faith upon which the church would be built (Matthew 16:13–20). But alongside this leadership was the craving for the respect of others that led him to rash declarations of self-importance, causing Jesus to rebuke him. ("You are not setting your mind on the things of God but on the things of man," Matthew 16:22–23.) Peter's three-time denial that he even knew Jesus at Jesus's trial serves as the most tragic example of the fear of man in the entire Bible. But Peter received the forgiveness of the risen Christ and the power of the Spirit. In this transforming conversion, he begins to see victory over his craving for the esteem of others. When he addresses the crowds on the day of Pentecost, he shows a dynamic trust in God in the face of a skeptical crowd (Acts 2:1–41). Later we see Peter's redeemed boldness before the Sanhedrin, when the apostles are commanded to stop preaching the gospel and Peter replies, "We must obey God rather than men" (Acts 5:29).

Peter's life was transformed from the fear of man into bold trust in the Lord. He knew he had been ransomed from futile ways by the precious blood of Christ (1 Peter 1:18–19). But Peter's story also reminds us that even someone who trusts in the Lord can be ensnared again by the fear of man. The apostle Paul writes in Galatians that Peter was justly rebuked because he "feared the circumcision party" in Antioch and compromised his principles as a result (Galatians 2:11–14). In the end, however, we see in Peter's life, teaching, and martyrdom a man who trusted the Lord and found ultimate release from the fear of man.

My own conversion to faith in Christ was marked by a sudden and profound release from the fear of man. From the first day of my walk with Christ, I experienced the disruption of all my close relationships, since my friends could not understand my abrupt change. Some friends were resentful that I no longer wanted to party with them the way I had. Others just simply became "unavailable" to my calls. It hurt, but the loss of status in my former world was a small cost for freedom in Christ. I also found my eyes and heart opened to people I would have never even noticed before. I was drawn in compassion toward people who didn't fit in. I didn't mind who I was seen with (or not seen with). When I placed my trust in the Lord, I found safety from the fear of man.

But the snare is never far away. I still love respect from those I respect. I still want to be popular and well-liked. If left to my own preferences, I will seek out relationships that make me feel good about myself and avoid relationships that require self-denial. I feel this almost daily as a pastor. The perks of ministry tend to be relational and social status perks, so they are an ongoing temptation to revert to the fear of man. The fear of man is deadly to all true Christian ministry. It's deadly for any endeavor that matters in life. If we are not alert to the snare of the fear of man, we can lose sight of what is most important about us—the fact that we belong to Christ. As Murray Harris notes, "Slavery to people's whims and fancies, to their requests and demands, compromises the prior and exclusive claim of Christ to the Christian's total devotion. Any slavery to people amounts to a repudiation of slavery to Christ."[2]

If you consider yourself a Christian, do you have any tendencies that reveal an ongoing vulnerability to the fear of man? Can you tell the difference between the approval trap and a healthy desire to make friends, fit in, and have others think well of you? Most important, do you know how to escape the snare of the fear of man to reach freedom and safety by trusting in the Lord? The approval trap can be a daily snare and it must be resisted through daily habit. Trust in the Lord is not a one-time remedy; it is a lifestyle of safety. Let me offer two lifelong pursuits that will help you resist the fear of man and keep you out of the approval trap.

LIVE LIKE YOU WERE BOUGHT BY CHRIST

In earlier chapters we learned that to be purchased for freedom is not to be granted free agency. Redemption releases us from the bondage of sin into the loving ownership of God. Those who live in daily awareness, gratitude, and wonder that they have been chosen and accepted by God through Christ will find, as George Whitefield once said, that "fear of man wears off daily."[3]

What difference would this truth make in someone like Ellen? Do you think it would help her the next time a guy wanted to entangle her in the web of his desires? What if she was able to fight the temptation to submerge her identity into a romantic relationship—what if she realized that no man has an inherent right to her since that right only belongs to God? What if she were able to respond to men's advances with the knowledge that she doesn't need their love, since the love of Christ has been poured into her heart through the Holy Spirit (Romans 5:5)? Knowing she belongs to God, she could begin to seek his will for her life, not the will of a man, a group, or her family. She could discover a dignity and purpose that didn't need the validation of others. And rather than carving out self-protecting boundaries, she could learn to wisely and sacrificially love others to promote their good in Christ, free of the need to be approved or appreciated. She could rebuild relationships in her family with a mature appreciation for who they are, because she knows who she is in Christ. Under the ownership of God, Ellen would learn to trust the Lord and experience his safety.

Where would Ellen learn and practice this kind of God-owned life? Ellen's thoughts and feelings have been totally skewed by the fear of man. She obsesses over what others think about her. As Welch said, people are big and God is not. How can that change? One way is through the regular spiritual practices of prayer and Bible reading. Taking time each day for regular biblical reflection and prayer is itself an act of trust in the Lord. It is a declaration of God's ownership over us and our need for his Word and grace if we are to live free of the fear of man. The more God's Word shapes our understanding of who we are and how we should live, the less the expectations of others will play that role. And prayer is where we actively engage the battle in our own hearts over what others think of us and want from us. Through prayer we align our wills with God's will (Jesus told us to pray "Your will be done" in Matthew 6:10), which effectively eliminates the will of others as the defining influence in our lives.

We all need to see others in correct proportion in this God-centered world. We need to see ourselves as free from others but owned by God. The spiritual disciplines are daily practices of that reality.

LIVE LIKE YOU BELONG AMONG THE PEOPLE OF GOD

Here's a surprising way to stay free of the approval trap. It comes from my own experience since I first acknowledged Christ as my Savior. Nothing has done more to help me live with people without fearing them than my involvement in a church community. And nothing has done more than the church to teach me how to trust the Lord in all my relationships.

Maybe your church experience doesn't inspire confidence in what I'm saying. I understand that. We all know how superficial people can seem in church. We've seen people put on the "church face" as they walk in the sanctuary. Christian cliques in the church can seem like the cliques we see everywhere else. We talk about love and brotherhood in our services, but we can live with judgment and favoritism everywhere else. So how can the church help us keep free of the approval trap?

First, let's remember what the church is in its essence. It isn't a club, a social group, or an organization. A local church is God's redeemed people, living in gospel community and gospel mission under the shepherding care of the Lord of the Church, Jesus Christ (see 1 Peter 2:9–10; 5:1–4). Though no church is perfect, this is what a true church is at its core. Church problems happen not because of what it is, but who it is. The "who" is you and me, sinners purchased by Christ's blood for freedom, and placed together in community for the sake of God's purposes. God forms disciples through the ministry of the church; he makes his presence known in and through the witness of the church; and he draws lost people to himself through the outreach of the church.

If you don't see your experience in church this way, let me ask you to try something. What if you set a goal to conquer the fear of man through your participation in the church? What might that look like? Maybe something like this:

You wake up on a Sunday morning and, rather than thinking about what you personally need from God that morning (though there's nothing wrong with that), you ask God to minister to you as part of the whole congregation. As you come into church, you don't look for friends or familiar faces first.

Instead, you look for someone who may be new, somebody you don't know. You introduce yourself and, just maybe, you become the first connection that person makes to the church. During the service, every time you sense that you are comparing yourself with others, or are tempted to judge others because they seem to put on a "church face" and don't seem real, you resist the temptation. You remind yourself of your own church face. You remember that others are more like you than they're different. You thank God for the redeeming grace that has brought you all together. As you sing, you resist the temptation to wonder how you look or sound and focus on the truths you are singing. You don't evaluate the preacher or sermon; instead, you listen for one or two things that will help you love God and others better. After the service, rather than immediately connecting with people you like, you look for a brother or sister who might need prayer or a word of encouragement.

This different way of life in the church begins to affect other contexts you're in. You go to small group looking to minister, not just to connect with friends or receive ministry. When you're in a group you think, *How can I help this interaction be a blessing for everyone?* rather than trying to make it serve your needs. You respect the church leaders but you don't allow the desire for their approval to shape the way you relate to them. When you see friends living in ways that are inconsistent with what they profess, you risk their disapproval and are willing to offer loving correction. If someone you feel is less gifted than you is given greater ministry opportunity, you remind yourself that we are all servants of Christ. You rejoice with the person and commit to encouraging her success. You offer yourself freely to others without expecting something in return.

You're starting to get the idea. Do you see how the church is ideally suited, in both its strengths and weaknesses, to help you learn to trust the Lord and overcome the fear of man? There is nowhere else where the gospel of redemption is proclaimed so frequently, where opportunities to apply it are made available so abundantly, and where the messiness of learning to trust God and not fear man can be worked out so constructively. The church is the company of people who belong to Christ trying to live that trust in Christ and love for others. That's the kind of place where the fear of man goes to die.

REDEMPTION AND THE TRAP OF EMOTIONAL ABUSE

Before concluding this chapter, I want to speak specifically to one terrible implication of the approval trap. That is emotional (or some use the term psychological) abuse. I'm not going to talk about physically abusive relationships—that is a topic I can't treat adequately here. But there are situations and relationships where one person (or persons) can exercise an inordinate level of control over others through the manipulation of fear or affection. This emotional abuse is a particularly dangerous form of the approval trap.

Emotional abuse is possible in any ongoing personal relationship. What is particularly challenging about it is that the person being abused often doesn't realize the trap he or she is in. Emotional abuse patterns often emerge subtly over time. What was once a "need for respect" can morph into a demand for subservience. Also, there are rarely outward traumatic events that bring emotional abuse into the light. People around the situation, and even the abused person, can adapt to the patterns of abuse and never see the warning signs when it is happening. Maybe most significantly, people who are emotional abusers develop finely honed instincts to control others with a variety of strategies that they employ as they feel the need.

For example, an emotional abuser may express great emotional neediness, using the compassion of a victim to draw her into a stifling sense of responsibility for the abuser's welfare. But if the victim begins to assert a sense of identity outside the relationship, the abuser may react in anger or jealousy, using fear and guilt to rope the victim back in. Accusations, belittling, and isolation are some common tactics in emotional abuse. Control tactics can be used that are calibrated to the victim's vulnerabilities—threats of self-harm, vague promises of abandonment, rejection, or retribution can all be used to keep a victim dependent on and subject to the desires of the abuser. The result is the manipulating control of one person over another, a toxic and destructive approval trap.

Ellen would come to see over time that she was particularly susceptible to emotional abuse. She was too ready to adapt her personality to the strong attentions of someone else. She so hated the idea of being rejected that she would do almost anything to hold onto a relationship. Like most emotional abuse victims, she would lose herself in the orbit of someone else and she couldn't see how trapped she was. She was not the perpetrator of the abuse; she was the victim. But victims are vulnerable to perpetrators, and for years she let the abuse cycle define her life.

If you are or have been the victim of emotional abuse or the oppressive control of someone else, please take time to carefully consider what follows: You do not belong to any person. No one has the right to determine who you are, what you think, feel, do, say, or who you choose to relate to in your life. The power to act on this will not come from within you. Liberty from the emotional abuse trap begins as you embrace the freedom that comes to you through the ownership of Christ. In the gospel, an abuse victim can find liberty because:

- You have been set free from the need to please and satisfy others, because your identity is not based on others' approval of your performance but on God's acceptance of you based on Christ's performance. Therefore, nobody has a right to define you or to demand that you conform to what they want you to be.
- Your responsibility to love, obey, and serve God determines and defines all other relationships. We love, not because others demand it of us, but because Christ first loved us (1 John 4:10–11). Therefore, nobody has the right to tell you what kind of relationship you should have with them.
- Any need to subordinate yourself in any relationship is limited by the primary call you have to hear and obey Christ. Therefore, you are accountable to God first and foremost. No one holds the key to your life but God.
- You are owned by God, bought with the precious blood of Jesus. You don't deserve his love, you didn't earn it, and you can't lose it. That is the most important and beautiful thing about you. Therefore, don't

let anyone rob you of it by emotional demands and manipulation. Loving others does not mean making them happy or keeping them satisfied. It means loving God and asking him to help you love others in ways that serve his interests in their lives.

If you know individuals who may be in an emotionally abusive situation, reach out to them with the gospel of redemption. Don't try to control them out of a controlling relationship. Help them to see who they are, or can be, in Christ. Help them discern what obedience to God's Word might look like. Support them if they decide to make tough biblical stands. They won't feel right about drawing appropriate lines and they may not do it well. But individuals who make the tough decision to follow Christ in the face of emotional manipulation need to know that there is a place where they will be safe. They need people around them who will recognize their vulnerabilities and not exert undue influence on them. You can be that person. Your church can be that place.

FREE, SAFE, AND SECURE

Do you struggle with the approval trap? I know I do. We are all like Ellen at times. The snare is never far away. But those who are free in Christ are free indeed. As nineteenth-century pastor Charles Bridges once declared,

> Fear brings us into the snare. Faith brings us liberty, safety, exaltation. Oh! Thou God of power and grace, may my soul praise thee for this mighty deliverance, this

joyous freedom! May I never be ashamed of my Master! May I be bound to his people, and glory in his cross![4]

Chapter 6

THE LAZINESS TRAP

Drew is stuck in the laziness trap. Compared to some of the traps we'll be talking about, the laziness trap may seem pretty benign. But in its own way, it ensnares and controls people in decades-long habits that can lay waste to potential in life. As one writer described it, "Laziness grows on people; it begins in cobwebs and ends in iron chains."[1] Anyone caught in the laziness trap knows its dark side, the gnawing despair of regret. A life of unfulfilled dreams, failed plans, and disappointed loved ones. True confession: I know the laziness trap inside and out. For years I wasted gifts and opportunities in the pursuit of comfort and ease. I can identify with Drew. I know many of you can too. The laziness trap is an easy one to fall into and a very difficult one to escape. Drew's story is my story.

If you observed my life over time, you might not have said, "That's a lazy guy." I was a busy pastor working six days a week, caring for the needs of hundreds of people along with the daily administrative tasks of running a church, with nary a golf outing in sight. I was a husband and father of four, riding herd on the competing agendas of church activities, school, sports, and the management of home and family life. On the surface I might have seemed busy, even productive. But the laziness trap had permeated my daily life.

If you were to come into the prison cell of my laziness, you would see the disarray of a life committed to procrastination. I survived college because the only class details that mattered were due dates and the day before due dates. Tardiness, a telltale sign of laziness, is a frontier I've spent a lifetime exploring. Lazy people love comfort and ease. In the early Christian era, monks used to talk about the "noontime demon"—the tendency to seek relaxation and ease when you should be working. I am very familiar with the noontime demon. I have *two* favorite recliners in my house—and one is right next to my bed.

Lazy people aren't very time-conscious. I can amuse and distract myself through a traffic jam or flight delay without any sense of lost time. It's not hard for me to identify with Mark Twain's description of himself: "I have seen slower people than I am—and more deliberate . . . and even more quieter, more listless, and lazier people than I am. But they were dead."[2]

The first time I was aware of my laziness, I was reading about the tree sloth (itself a revealing window into my endless distractibility). I discovered that what the tree sloth does best is sleep. I love to sleep; in fact, it may be the thing I do best. I can sleep almost anywhere, any time. I once experimented to see how comfortable I could make myself in the dentist's chair. The next thing I knew, I had fallen asleep *to the grinding sound of a dental drill in my mouth!* Anyway, back to the sloth. The only time he stirs is when the craving for food becomes stronger than the craving for sleep. Me too! If left alone, sloths are not unpleasant. Check. They have a good sense of smell but they don't hear well. Verified by my wife. The sloth's main defense against predators is its almost constant inactivity. In the wild they are often mistaken for a big pile of dead leaves. Inadvertently I had discovered the answer to the party question, "If you were an animal, what kind of animal would you be?"

Sensing the uncomfortable prodding of the Holy Spirit, I decided to study the issue of sloth. Some unfamiliar terms emerged from my study. My leafy spirit animal was called the sloth after the Old English word for "slowness." Slothfulness has been defined as "habitual disinclination to exertion." A lazy person is also known as a sluggard. Synonyms include such unappealing terms as "ne'er-do-well," "layabout," "idler," "loafer," and "slacker." Alongside these pejorative synonyms were such wonderfully descriptive terms as "indolence" (causing no pain and relatively benign), "inertia" ("having no inherent power of action, motion, or resistance"—been there, done that!), and my favorite, "torpor" or "torpidity" (a term meaning lethargic indifference). I confess I have lived a life of torpor. But I still didn't see big problems with it.

EVERYBODY LOVES A SLUGGARD

I think I've discovered some reasons why sloth fails to register on the dysfunction meter. For one, sluggards rarely instigate conflict. You won't see a sluggard rant, verbally attack, or make outrageous demands. Conflict is just something else to be avoided. I'd rather let you win an argument than put in the effort to win it myself.

In addition, the sluggard is almost by definition dull to his problems. Sluggards are habitual escape artists. Find a sluggard and you'll find someone with a highly developed skill and appetite for leisure and diversion. The ability to divert stress into distraction can come in handy in some ways. I don't worry a whole lot. I don't tend to carry grudges—too much work. But I can be very dull to the needs of others. The trap of laziness lulls us into assuming that everything around us is okay, or at least it will be if we avoid it long enough. You can't be lazy without being inherently selfish. I began to see the problem but still couldn't see the destructive power of its trap.

THE OUTER RUIN OF THE SLUGGARD'S LIFE

I turned to the Bible for insight into my sluggardly tendencies. The Scriptures, particularly the book of Proverbs, speak with penetrating straightforwardness to the laziness trap. The first thing I noticed is that nearly all the proverbs related to laziness or slothfulness show up more than once. That's probably a tip-off on how dense laziness can make us.

The sluggard—the lazy man—is a familiar character in the book of Proverbs. He is a tragi-comic figure, as you can see from this group of sayings:

The sluggard says, "There is a lion in the road!
There is a lion in the streets!"
As a door turns on its hinges,
so does a sluggard on his bed.
The sluggard buries his hand in the dish;
it wears him out to bring it back to his mouth.
(Proverbs 26:13–15)

The sluggard is often contrasted with the diligent, whose industry is consistently characterized as an expression of wisdom in Proverbs. As Old Testament scholar Tremper Longman notes, "In Proverbs, laziness is seen as the epitome of foolish behavior."[3] The book of Proverbs offers no hope for the sluggard. He is destined to a life of foolish waste and could-have-beens. His life matters little to others, except perhaps as a nuisance or object lesson.

The sluggard is a fool ambling aimlessly along at a slacker's pace. And this is where it gets serious. Foolishness in the Bible is a category of sin, an expression of living absent the fear of God. So the sluggard is burdened by more than selfishness. He is burdened by sin. The laziness trap is far more spiritually deadly than we might imagine.

By looking at some particular proverbs related to sloth, you can see the long-term damage to a life caught in the laziness trap. Consider the following clusters of proverbs and the implications they raise for your life.

THE DAMAGE OF FRUITLESSNESS

> The soul of the sluggard craves and gets nothing,
> while the soul of the diligent is richly supplied.
> (Proverbs 13:4)

> The sluggard does not plow in the autumn;
> he will seek at harvest and have nothing. (Proverbs 20:4)

This is another way of looking at procrastination. If you are a chronic procrastinator, you know the experience of lowering your standards when you don't do what you set out to do. You know what it's like to fret over the "could haves, should haves, would haves" of life. You know what it's like to come to harvest time and have nothing.

THE DAMAGE OF FITFULNESS

> The way of a sluggard is like a hedge of thorns,
> but the path of the upright is a level highway.
>   (Proverbs 15:19)

> The desire of the sluggard kills him,
> for his hands refuse to labor. (Proverbs 21:25)

Are you a pressure avoider? One thing I noticed about myself was how much of a "big push, no finish" life I lived. I was always making resolutions, turning over new leaves, rolling up my sleeves, but rarely truly seeing change. I began to realize that my big-push efforts were primarily intended to get whatever was pressuring me far enough away so that I could return to my normal gear of lazy life.

THE DAMAGE OF FAITHLESSNESS

> Like vinegar to the teeth and smoke to the eyes,
> so is the sluggard to those who send him. (Proverbs
>   10:26)

> The sluggard is wiser in his own eyes
> than seven men who can answer sensibly.
>   (Proverbs 26:16)

Does your laziness tend to have a Drew effect on others? If you are married, has your spouse adopted a work-around approach to life with you? If you are a parent, are your children accustomed to accepting your "meant well" for what should be a "did well"? Have those around you simply lowered their expectations for what you will deliver on your promises? Far from being a victimless crime, sloth steadily erodes others' confidence in us. In so doing, it shrivels the potential for our godly influence in their lives as well.

Proverbs provides us with pithy but penetrating diagnostic pictures that can and should bring our laziness into the light. One particular section of Proverbs was most helpful in battling the sin of sloth in my life.

> I passed by the field of a sluggard,
> by the vineyard of a man lacking sense,
> and behold, it was all overgrown with thorns;
> the ground was covered with nettles,
> and its stone wall was broken down.
> Then I saw and considered it;
> I looked and received instruction.
> A little sleep, a little slumber,
> a little folding of the hands to rest,
> and poverty will come upon you like a robber,
> and want like an armed man. (Proverbs 24:30–34)

These proverbs are an extended meditation on the life of the sluggard. It is almost as if a father is taking a child on a field trip, pointing out wisdom and foolishness in the world around. As they pass the field of the sluggard, he stops and gives a chilling and sober warning from this visual parable.

He notes the field: It is evidently a prized piece of property, walled around and used for the highest-value cash crop in the economy, a vineyard. But rather than seeing well-tended rows of grapes, he sees weeds and thorns, and a wall falling down through disrepair. It is a sad and wasteful sight, made all the more tragic by the fact that the owner is apparently somewhere nearby. The problem with this field is not that it has been abandoned by an absentee owner. It has been neglected by someone nearby who seems oblivious to the loss he is incurring—because he is more concerned with his ease than his responsibility. What is the foolishness of the sluggard? The sluggard has something good (his field) and he doesn't protect it. Not only that, he wastes the potential of his field. The result is that where he should have something, he has nothing—and that's foolish.

In the southeast US where I grew up, there is a vine called kudzu, which was initially imported from Asia because it was fast-growing and could prevent soil erosion. But kudzu is considered a nuisance now, because whatever positive characteristics it brings, the negatives far outweigh its usefulness. Kudzu grows rapidly, a foot a day, and is very difficult to eradicate once it roots. Left untended, it will take over everything—trees, power lines, road signs, houses. It is not unusual to drive along the highways and back roads of the Deep South and see kudzu blanketing every inch of what was formerly a productive property. You don't really think about it until you see the damage done. Like kudzu, slothfulness doesn't shock us until we see what it destroys.

What is the take-home point from this visit to the wasted field? "A little sleep, a little slumber, a little folding of the hands to rest, and poverty will come on you like a bandit and want like an armed man" (vv. 33–34). The wise teacher indicates the bottom line: Whether you lose something by violent crime or lazy indifference, whether it is taken suddenly or dwindles slowly over time, when it's gone, it's gone. This is where I saw the real tragedy of the laziness trap. When sloth rules our hearts, poverty eventually rules our lives. The warning of Proverbs 24:30–34 continues to serve its purpose in my life—a loss that doesn't need to happen, but is possible with a little chronic folding of my hands to rest.

THE INNER REBELLION OF THE SLUGGARD'S LIFE

Still, it's one thing to see the bad effect of sloth and another to trace that bad effect to the sin in my heart, the place where all traps need to be addressed. Sloth simply never feels like sin to me—it just feels like my personality. So I began to ask the Lord to show me the willful sin in it. Not simply the consequences, but the devoted idolatry that must be underneath the easygoing lifestyle. Keying off Proverbs, I began to consider the fact that the sluggard doesn't really submit to anybody. He might go along, might not raise a ruckus, but he's not going to yield his way of doing life to anyone for anything. He is—I am—a passive rebel. With this thought in mind, I've developed this personal definition of sloth.

> Spiritual sloth is a determined bent of my heart that stubbornly insists on its own way. It is aggressive disobedience to God's rule through passive means. It is a trap that demands I sacrifice what's best for what's most comfortable. Laziness is a daily bondage that, if not fought, will leave

me uninspired by, and therefore unprepared for, the adventure of faith.

Perhaps nobody ever embodied the willful trap of sloth like Bartleby the Scrivener. I first read this classic Herman Melville short story in high school and it unsettled me for reasons I couldn't understand at the time. I happened to pick it up and read it again during my study on sloth and God used it to profoundly confront my heart.

The story is set in New York during the 1800s. The title character is a law office clerk, one whose skill is making handwritten copies of legal documents. When he is first hired, Bartleby is a fine addition to the office, performing his job well. But as his employer (who narrates the story) begins to discover, Bartleby is very diligent in the things he wants to do, but increasingly resistant to requests to do anything else. His reply to any request outside his preference is a pleasant, "I prefer not to." At first this is seen as a quirk in an otherwise diligent employee. But soon the employer finds that Bartleby *only* does what he wants to do, and his myopic commitment to that end pits him in a battle of wits and wills with his employer. Bartleby never attacks, but his obsession with what he wants to do ultimately dominates everything and everyone around him. He simply will not give over his right to do what he wants, no matter what the consequence. Unable to persuade Bartleby to do anything other than what he prefers, the owner eventually moves the business itself, leaving Bartleby just as he wants to be. The story ends with Bartleby in a shelter for vagrants called the Tombs, where his life ebbs away to nothing. The final scene has the employer stooped over the wasted life of a man who did what he preferred but lost everything in the process.

"I prefer not to." It's one thing to say it to a boss. It's another thing entirely to take this posture in the face of the Holy God and Ruler of the Cosmos. Yet it is so familiar; I've said the same thing with my words and actions a thousand different ways. Through the lens of Scripture we see that Bartleby's chief problem is sloth—evil rebellion masked in benign preferences. I know Bartleby in my soul. What I need is a different way to live.

Philosopher Paul Maxwell has said it well. "Before we can escape patterns of laziness, we need to understand patterns of laziness: We're shackled by cycles of sin—retreat and repeat—and they're not easy to escape. We need to know what we need—where and how God's grace comes to the lazy man."[4]

I've learned that this grace comes to redeem us from the trap of sinful, rebellious laziness into the loving rule of Christ. Here's how I got there.

THE SLUGGARD MEETS THE SAVIOR

Let's suppose Drew has seen the foolish behaviors in his sloth. He's explored the cycle of folly that sloth produces. And he has seen the roots of self-absorption and rebellion that drove him into the trap of laziness. How does he change? First, he needs to anchor his hope in the truth of his redemption. Jesus Christ left eternal bliss to take on human form and spill his blood to ransom Drew. He has taken Drew from the field of thorns and lost potential and brought him into a new field to cultivate new fruit. What about that field? The writer of Hebrews walks us past it.

> Land that has drunk the rain that often falls on it, and produces a crop useful to those for whose sake it is cultivated, receives a blessing from God. But if it bears thorns and thistles, it is worthless and near to being cursed, and its end is to be burned. Though we speak in this way, yet in your case, beloved, we feel sure of better things— things that belong to salvation. For God is not unjust so as to overlook your work and the love that you have shown for his name in serving the saints, as you still do. And we desire each one of you to show the same earnestness to have the full assurance of hope until the end, so that you may not be sluggish, but imitators of those who through faith and patience inherit the promises. (Hebrews 6:7–12)

This is a wonderful contrast passage to Proverbs 24. Here we see a field blessed by God. The possibility of the sluggard's wasted field still exists, but it need not be the case (vv. 7–8). There are no encouragements in Proverbs for the sluggard, but here we find confident encouragement that things will be different because they are "things that belong to salvation." Though we have been sluggards in the flesh, the redemptive work of God transforms our lives and sets us on the path of salvation (v. 9). We see that God recognizes the faith of his redeemed people as true faith and the love of his redeemed people as true love. God gives good fields for us to till and promises the blessing of good fruit. These promises are activated because we have been redeemed from the tyranny of self and supplied with grace working itself out in diligence from the heart.

Grace is the answer to sloth because grace is antithetical to sloth. It is God working in us to be diligent, and us working out our salvation by grace (Philippians 2:12–13). This grace is reality-based. It doesn't deny the temptation for us to turn away from working grace to laziness. We need not live in fear of failure. Instead, as we look around us among the free people of God, we find courage to persevere in diligence (v. 12). We have inherited fields filled with great promise—fields of mission, fields of family, fields of ministry, vocation, talent, and gifting. God's grace works to make us diligent to tend these fields with the promise of his blessing always in view. We work against laziness and procrastination because we want to bring honor to the One who not only owns the field, but who owns us as well.

LAZY PEOPLE CAN CHANGE

I distinctly remember a time when I confronted the thing spiritually-minded lazy people fear most—repentance. Repentance is not what we do to right ourselves with God. That's been done for us by Jesus. Repentance is what we do when we are right with God. It is change in the direction of obedience toward what God desires for us. Repentance is intentional, grace-empowered change over time. Lazy people don't like focused effort over time toward much of anything. We'd prefer not to. But I came across a simple, straightforward verse in Scripture that galvanized faith in my heart for change and gave me an open pathway out of the laziness trap.

> Do not be slothful in zeal, be fervent in spirit, serve the Lord. (Romans 12:11)

This verse provides me with a targeted "put-off," a challenging "put-on," and a new sense of identity that all work together against my lifelong habits of laziness.

The "put-off" is expressed in a negative—"Do not be slothful in zeal." The gospel produces people who are ruined for anything less than what God has for them in Christ. Our passions (zeal) can only be satisfied in God himself. The slothful "I prefer not to" needs to be seen as the opposite of godly zeal. This isn't a one-time commitment to bold living. Been there and done that. It is a daily fight to "not be slothful in zeal." Sometimes the difference between sloth and zeal is whether I watch one football game and then engage my family, or whether I watch a football game and then take a nap. Or whether I pick up a book or the remote. Or do my work or surf the net. Go over and talk to my neighbor or just wave and go inside my house. It's in those little daily "put-offs" that the battle for zeal rages. While zeal for the Lord is never a natural state, it is always bubbling up from grace. According to Paul, we don't need to go looking for it; we just need to stop quenching it. By God's grace, I can do that.

The "put-on" involves keeping my spiritual fervor. One older commentary says, "A fervent spirit is the reverse of sloth, and always prompts to diligence and vigor of action. Christians ought to possess such a spirit in doing all their business, especially in the things of the Lord."[5] This is where I have found the habit of reading so helpful. These days we seem to have lost the art of reading for spiritual growth. We look for things that entertain us or comfort us in our struggles. But how many people give the time and focus to reading books simply for the goal of stirring spiritual fervor? We have been trained by a daily diet of social media to demand that the things we read scratch an immediate itch. I'm conscious of that even as I'm writing this book. I know that there are people who will be tempted to put this book down if it doesn't seem immediately relevant to a pressing sense of need. Or if it doesn't have compelling stories and illustrations.

I understand that—it's my job as an author to make a book readable. Now, this isn't an appeal to keep reading this book. It *is* an appeal to rethink how you read. To commit yourself to reading hard things, important things, things that will cause you to think more about God and less about you. I find that people who read well in this way tend to be fervent in spirit even in dry or difficult seasons of their spiritual journey. There are excellent books all around us that will help us—some are hundreds of years old, some came out this year. Read selectively. Read thoughtfully. Read aggressively. But read to stay fervent in spirit.

The last phrase urges me to "serve the Lord." The great deception of the laziness trap is that it promises freedom. "I prefer not to" comes with an implied "because." As in, "because what I want for me is best." The promise of freedom that the laziness trap offers is really the snare of worldly and fleshly self-comfort and self-absorption. But the apostle Paul exposes this snare and offers a different way of freedom. "For you were called to freedom, brothers. Only do not use your freedom as an opportunity for the flesh, but through love serve one another" (Galatians 5:13).

This is an action, but it begins with a frame of mind— an identity. We learned in chapter 4 that "serving" language is better understood as "slavery" language. A slave is not a consultant, not a union worker, not a free agent, not a partner. A slave is the property of another, purchased to do his will and represent his interests. When I consider "I prefer not to" in light of my status as a redeemed servant of the Lord Jesus Christ, it is a ludicrous thought. What is there that Christ has not given me? What do I have that he does not truly own? My time, my possessions, my rights? The glory of redemption is not that we are simply freed from sin. It is that we become property of the True Master. It is to belong, to have an identity and a status. Yes, it is as a servant, but what glory is that servitude! As John Stott writes, "True freedom is not freedom from responsibility to God and others in order to live for ourselves, but freedom from ourselves in order to live for God and others."[6]

The way to stay out of the laziness trap is to stay in the servant mind-set. Servants don't procrastinate; they are busy with the work the Master has given them to do. Servants see time as valuable because it is a gift, and they want to use it wisely. They see their gifts and talents as tools to be developed and deployed to tend the field they have been given. A servant knows how to rest, but has learned the difference between rest and endless distraction. Rather than say with Bartleby the Scrivener, "I prefer not to," servants say with John Newton, "What Thou wilt; when Thou wilt; how Thou wilt."[7]

Perhaps most significantly, the servant knows that his or her time on earth is not for long. The rewards of sloth, such as they are, all take place in this life. The rewards of the servant begin in this life but shower down in glory. What has changed my life and freed me from the trap of laziness is a revolution of redemption. More and more I want the distractions of this world to entice me less, and the hopes of heaven to entice me more. Do you want this as well?

In the last sentence of his preface to his autobiography, *Grace Abounding to the Chief of Sinners*, John Bunyan issued a call to those who want to live for God's glory in this world in anticipation of eternal glory in the world to come: "My dear children. The milk and honey is beyond this wilderness. God be merciful to you, and grant that you be not slothful to go in to possess the land."[8]

May we have such a vision, and live in the good of it. Let's never be slothful in zeal, but be fervent in spirit to serve the Lord.

Chapter 7

THE TRAP OF SECRET ESCAPE

In chapter 1 we encountered two people, Maria and Steven, who are living double lives. Maria is living in bondage to an eating disorder. Steven is trapped by chronic pornography use. Maybe they sit near each other in church, or in adjacent cubicles at work. They may be friends. But neither Maria nor Steven has any idea of the dark places where the other spends so much time. The things that ensnare them—food and sex—are around them all the time. To others, they are the stuff of the good life. To Maria and Steven, they are merciless chains of secret escape.

WHAT IS A SECRET ESCAPE?

In this chapter we're going to address what I call the trap of secret escape. We'll be looking at two particular ways normal physical desires can be misused and perverted to dangerous extremes.

There are two questions to address right off the bat. First, what do I mean by "secret escape"? We all face temptations to look for some kind of escape or diversion when dealing with the stress and disappointments of life. There are healthy ways to cope, things like sports, music, hobbies, and social activities. But there are unhealthy escapes as well. Maria and Steven have created their own private worlds of indulgence that offer satisfaction or release that nothing else in life seems to give. These escapes draw them inward on themselves, providing a refuge that they can indulge whenever they want.

Secret escapes are enticing because they provide both intense pleasure and immediate distraction at the same time. But what begins as an occasional pursuit of release and relief can escalate into a life-dominating compulsion to indulge or purge yourself in private orgies of lust or food obsession. This private world becomes a trap that can have horribly destructive consequences. That's what I mean by the trap of secret escape.

The second question is probably something like this: "Are you really going to address eating disorders and pornography in the same chapter?" Valid question. Most likely, if you have read anything on eating disorders, it has been written by a woman for women. And if you've read anything on pornography, it has been written by a man for men. That makes sense because statistics show that the overwhelming majority of people struggling with eating disorders are women and the overwhelming majority of people using pornography are men.

But I'm going to make the somewhat unorthodox point that these two traps are actually in the same cell block of the prison we've been exploring. Looking at their commonalities, we can get underneath them a bit to learn how to get free from them. First, I need to state my case. Why do I think we can address eating disorders and pornography in the same discussion? I can't point to extensive surveys or studies that have explored this connection. As far as I've been able to research, no one has taken that on. But brain studies seem to show that various kinds of activities interact with the pleasure centers of the brain in overlapping ways. Food and sex are both powerful natural stimulators to these "binge centers" and seem to affect brain chemistry in similar ways.[1]

There is some sociological evidence as well. An interesting statistic has to do with the number of people who struggle with eating disorders or life-dominating pornography habits. Though it is difficult to obtain detailed data through statistical studies on these behaviors, it does appear that roughly the same number of men struggle with porn as women who struggle with eating disorders. With a US population that is roughly half male and half female, this seems to indicate some sort of mirroring effect of these disorders in our culture.

Psychologically, there are some remarkable similarities between eating disorders and pornography use. Both are intensely personal, isolating, and anonymous behaviors. That's why they are secret escapes; they demand a person withdraw from social environments and relational connections in order to pursue them. They are both intensely sensual and physical. It's not wrong to describe food and sex as appetites, even needs, that can be pursued in healthy ways or abused in unhealthy ways. Both struggles are most commonly connected to visual imagery, particularly an idealized image of the female body. Our culture's tragic exploitation of women has led to unattainable standards of the feminine form that ensnare the imaginations of women and men in different ways. For Maria, impossibly thin and airbrushed images of women on fashion runways and in magazine layouts mock her for the relative inadequacy of her appearance, and she lives in bondage to the standard they set. For Steven, the alluring images of provocative, voluptuous women beckoned him into a sexual fantasy where he could do whatever he wanted. Both eating disorders and pornography find their entrapping power in unattainable cultural idols of beauty, power, and desire.

Eating disorders and pornography seem to offer similar escape value to men and women. People who find present life painful or disappointing escape into a fantasy world of illicit pleasures where they determine what they experience and feel whenever they want. Underneath both eating disorders and pornography fixation is a craving for some sort of control through escape. But that is the snare, because control is illusory and those who escape in this way have to eventually return to the world of real life that will never offer what escape seems to promise.

The common experience in both eating disorders and pornography is desensitization: the more food or sex matters, the less food or sex satisfies. The deeper a bulimic or anorexic goes into an eating disorder, the more physically damaging the habit becomes. Eating disorders are truly deadly traps. The danger in pornography is more in its collateral damage. As deeper and more perverse pornography is pursued, the possibilities of a ruined marriage, prostitution, predatory actions, and sexual abuse bring harsh reality crashing into a fantasy world. Tragically, costs to personal health, damage to personal relationships, or even legal implications don't keep people from running to their secret escapes. They have lost control and become prisoners of the traps they have created.

I began to see this connection between eating disorders and pornography in my counseling experience. I was meeting with a couple, Dale and Connie, whose marriage was in crisis after Dale's pornography compulsion had come to light. Connie was understandably horrified at the revelations.

"How could he do this to our marriage? Why wouldn't he tell me he was struggling? What does this say about me? What does it mean for our future?"

As these questions poured out in a torrent of tears, I tried to think of some way to help Connie at least comprehend Dale's struggle. Almost in desperation I asked if she had ever known a woman who had struggled with an eating disorder. Her sister Ann had a long battle with anorexia after a traumatic experience in college. Ann had hidden her problem for years, had denied it when confronted, and only began to get help when her health began to decline. It was devastating to the family, but they had rallied around Ann and not only helped her to work toward healthy eating habits, but supported her in the underlying emotional struggle to overcome the memories that shaped her view of herself.

As we talked about that experience, Connie gained some insight into her husband's problem. She began to see how, for Dale, pornography was only partly about sex, just as Ann's eating disorder was only partly about food. It gave her words to talk to Dale about his problem. They were able to talk about Dale's feelings of failure as a husband and father and his frustrations with work that tempted him to seek escape. Over time

Connie was able to battle through her disgust and shame to help her husband fight against porn.

I wondered if this was true for men as well. I have had opportunity to meet with couples where the wives were struggling with eating disorders. Husbands were frustrated that nothing they said seemed to help their wives feel better about their body image or eat in healthy ways. I began to help the husbands consider the powerful hold pornography can have in a man's life; how sexual cravings combine with shame to form a sinkhole that draws men into compulsive and destructive habits. Through this lens, they were able to see their wives' irrational fixations on food and diet with greater compassion, and to care for them with greater sensitivity and patience.

A CURRENT CRISIS WITH A TIMELESS ANSWER

We started this chapter talking about Maria and Steven. But from here on out, I'm going to let them step aside so I can talk directly to you.

What would you say if I told you that the Bible seems to confirm the connection between the wrong use of food and the wrong use of sex? Consider the words of the apostle Paul:

> "All things are lawful for me," but not all things are helpful. "All things are lawful for me," but I will not be dominated by anything. "Food is meant for the stomach and the stomach for food"—and God will destroy both one and the other. The body is not meant for sexual immorality, but for the Lord, and the Lord for the body. (1 Corinthians 6:12–13)

If you struggle with an eating disorder or with pornography, please hear what Paul is saying. You didn't get where you are now because one day you decided, "I want to spend my life in bingeing and purging" or "I want to use the pornographic exploitation of women to make me feel better." You have gotten to this tragic place because you made your own god out of something that cannot give you what you demand of it. That god offers you a sanctuary of secret escape, which is really just a trap. You thought you were getting relief or satisfaction by feeding on food or lust. But you have been feeding on yourself, and now that false god dominates you. Food or porn now rules you.

If you sought refuge through food or sex and now find yourself trapped in the very thing you thought would be an escape, there is wonderful news. Paul points the way out of the trap just a few verses later.

> Do you not know that your body is a temple of the Holy Spirit within you, whom you have from God? You are not your own, for you were bought with a price. So glorify God in your body. (1 Corinthians 6:19–20)

Elyse Fitzpatrick, a counselor who specializes in helping women with eating disorders, brings redemption into clear focus for those trapped in secret escape.

> How is it that God has claimed the right to ownership of your body? And what was the cost of this purchase? We who are Christians have been ransomed or purchased by the sacred blood of Jesus Christ, the Son of God. It benefits us, when thinking about the cost to God for us,

to take ourselves back to Calvary, back to the cross, where our precious, loving Lord suffered and died. Because Jesus paid such a price, not only for our bodies but also for our souls, we should seek to exalt Him in everything. We should not allow any sin to defile the sanctuary where He has chosen, by His Spirit, to reside.[2]

Do you see that? The craving for food or sex may seek mastery over you, but you can be set free. If you have received redemption in Christ, your body doesn't belong to food or sex. It doesn't even belong to you. It was bought with the ransom blood of Jesus! Your body has become a temple for the worship of God. Jesus has sent his Spirit to cleanse the temple of its defiling lusts and habits and set up a worship life within you that befits your new owner.

How does this happen? How can someone trapped in secret escape learn to live a life of freedom and worship?

I want to take the remainder of this chapter to walk you through a journey of liberation from the trap of secret escape. We're going to do that through a verse-by-verse application of Psalm 130. My hope is that, in this short but deeply resonant psalm, you'll find transformational truth for your struggles with food or sex, no matter how deep in the trap you find yourself.

Take a moment to read the psalm through. Then we'll apply it to your struggle.

Psalm 130: A Song of Ascents

Out of the depths I cry to you, O LORD!
2 O Lord, hear my voice!
Let your ears be attentive
to the voice of my pleas for mercy!

3 If you, O Lord, should mark iniquities,
O Lord, who could stand?
4 But with you there is forgiveness,
that you may be feared.

5 I wait for the LORD, my soul waits,
and in his word I hope;
6 my soul waits for the Lord
more than watchmen for the morning,
more than watchmen for the morning.

7 O Israel, hope in the LORD!
For with the LORD there is steadfast love,
and with him is plentiful redemption.
8 And he will redeem Israel
from all his iniquities.

ASCENT FROM THE ABYSS

The first thing you notice about this psalm is its title: "A Song of Ascents." This is one of fifteen psalms (Psalms 120—134) that are called Psalms of Ascents. Tradition indicates that they were grouped together and named this way because they were meant to be sung as pilgrims traveled on the road to the temple in Jerusalem for one of the great feasts of Israel. They are "traveling songs" for people looking to meet with God. Remember how we encountered Jesus in chapter 3? It is very likely that the disciples sang these songs as they walked with Jesus on the road to Jerusalem in Mark 10.

This particular song of ascent is unique in that it is the only one that is also a song of confession or penitence. The travelers singing this song don't believe that they have any right in themselves to meet with God. In fact, everything in them tells them to run away from him. Their awareness of their sinfulness and unworthiness is expressed in the repetition of references to God. Eight times in eight short verses we see attention drawn to God. The singers of this song are confessing more than disgust in themselves or shame over moral failure. They see their sin in light of God's holiness. They know that sin had cut them off from God and the only thing they deserved was his punishment.

Do you feel this way? Maria and Steven know the dark depths of bondage to a secret escape. Are you hopeless as you look at your willful and habitual commitment to things even you find revolting? Is God in the picture for you? If not, that's where you need to make your first adjustment. You'll never find the will or power to change if you don't reckon with the God who sees you in your secret escape and knows everything that happens there.

> Out of the depths I cry to you, O Lord! O Lord, hear my voice! Let your ears be attentive to the voice of my pleas for mercy! (vv. 1–2)

How bad does it get for you? How far have you gone into dark desires and self-degrading acts in your secret escape? Picture yourself there in that worst place, maybe even a little beyond that. And then ponder this: Even in that place you can cry out to God—and he will listen to you! That moment when the craving to purge is driving you to the bathroom—even after that. You can cry out and God will listen. That moment when you've fully committed to pleasuring yourself—even after that, you can cry out and God will listen. Kneeling and retching over that toilet, clicking madly through those obscene images, sitting alone in the dark in the depths of self-condemnation and hopelessness, out of the depths you can cry, and the Lord will hear your voice. Every time. God is not waiting for you to get willpower, to show some measure of self-respect, to come to your senses. Cry out. He is not far from you. He is a God of mercy.

> If you, O LORD, should mark iniquities, O Lord, who could stand? But with you there is forgiveness, that you may be feared. (vv. 3–4)

There is no escaping it. The massive mound of sin and self that you have built as you dug your hole of secret escape is not going anywhere. You know with glaring clarity the lies you've been weaving, the war you've waged against your own body, the voyeuristic exploitation of people you will never meet, the prostitution of your soul to the god of food or sex. Is there a chance that the God you cry out to might not see all this? Might choose to relate to you based on all the good you do when you aren't doing bad? There is no chance! The question the psalmist asks is rhetorical. God does indeed mark every sin. And it is good that he knows every ugly one of them. Because his response to your sin is complete forgiveness. Not forgiveness for just the ugly sins, not just the obvious ones. Those resentments and angry thoughts that feed your compulsion need forgiveness as well. The judgment and envy and coveting that turn you away from loving others to pleasuring yourself need forgiveness. The hiding, the self-pity, the fantasies, and the wasted hours in your secret escape need forgiveness. So do your many futile attempts at self-atonement. Through the redeeming blood of Jesus Christ, there is forgiveness for all of it. "In him we have redemption through his blood, the forgiveness of our trespasses, according to the riches of his grace" (Ephesians 1:7).

Why such amazing grace? So that God may be feared. "Oh, great, I get it. God wants to free me from this trap to get me under his thumb. What good is that?" Friend, when the psalmist uses the word "fear," there is nothing negative about it. When the psalmist ponders the fear of God, what comes to his mind is a path of wisdom (Proverbs 1:7), a fountain of life (Proverbs 14:27), abundant goodness and security (Psalm 31:19), divine protection, deliverance, and provision (Psalm 34:7–9). The fear of the Lord is simply the desire to live like those who have been bought with a price, to glorify God with everything about us. Over time the fear of God will begin to overwrite the corrupted thinking, feeling, and craving patterns that drive you to secret escapes with fresh desires to live free in Christ. Believe me, there is nothing that will turn you from lust for food or sex like the gracious fear of the Lord.

> I wait for the LORD, my soul waits, and in his word I hope; my soul waits for the Lord more than watchmen for the morning, more than watchmen for the morning. (vv. 5–6)

What if you do what the psalmist says and cry out from the depths? What happens next? Practically speaking, you have done one of the most important things you can ever do. You've stopped your headlong dive into escape and made a rational decision to deny your cravings and look to God. That is huge! What will happen next? Will your mind fill with spiritual visions? Will a committee of angels descend and carry you away from your temptation to a happy place? Not likely. This is where many sincere efforts to flee the trap of secret escape fail. You extract yourself from temptation but in your heart you continue to long for the thing that sent you there in the first place. Just because you're not bingeing and purging doesn't mean you don't envy the body of a supermodel. Just because you're not masturbating doesn't mean you're not lusting after the body of a porn star. The psalmist wants more than just to stop the bad. He wants better. Do you?

The psalmist knows he has to place his desires on new things. And so he places them on the word of hope. This is a time-release way of life; it doesn't come all at once. In your secret escape, you gave full-bodied devotion to the thing that offered relief from specific temptations and pain. As much as you'd like to tell yourself that you just fell into it, it was intentional action that got you into that secret place of escape. If pressed, most people who live in food or sex escapes can describe rituals and thinking patterns that get them where they want to go when they want to get there. But you must come to your senses and realize that "the end of those things is death" (Romans 6:21). There is no escape, only a trap.

So instead of escaping, you wait on God. Waiting on God means cultivating new ways of thinking about your life, ways that begin with believing that Jesus has purchased you out of the bondage of your escape trap to live in freedom with him.

The Holy Spirit will use that gospel truth to begin a renewal of your thinking about yourself and the world around you. That leads, over time, to new ways of responding to the stuff that used to send you running to your secret escape. New God-pleasing intentions, actions, and patterns will begin to take root in your life. Rather than serving as an escape into self, they will serve as a practice of hope.

What patterns and intentional actions can you see yourself doing? Have you withdrawn from real relationships into fantasy or isolation? How can you begin to reengage with real people? Has God's Word been set aside in favor of tempting images? How can you change that pattern? Do some of your new actions need to be radical for a time—like getting rid of a smartphone or a data plan? Do you need to meet with a nutritionist who can help you set a healthy food intake and monitor your progress? Do you need to open up in confession to your spouse, your friends? Do you need to get help and accountability in counseling or small groups? Are there opportunities to serve others that will help you keep from habitually serving yourself?

Why does the psalmist compare this activity to a watchman waiting for the morning—twice? It is a powerful, poetic image that would resonate with those who read his words. Watchmen stood on the walls of the city at night, peering into the darkness, looking for potential invaders. It was not work for slackers or the easily distracted. A watchman might go months or even years without seeing anything noteworthy. But God forbid if he were not at his post at the one time where true danger approached. What every watchman looked forward to was the dawning rays of the sun. They knew that if they saw the morning, then the night had gone well and they could rest.

You want to be that kind of watchman. Actively waiting for the Lord to work in your life will cut against every self-indulgent, self-medicating instinct you've had. There will be times when minutes will feel like hours and every breath you take will seem like a fight against the darkness. But keep looking out toward the horizon of hope. The light is coming for you. Daybreak is not far off. Stand your post and see the deliverance of God.

> O Israel, hope in the LORD! For with the LORD there is steadfast love, and with him is plentiful redemption. And he will redeem Israel from all his iniquities. (vv. 7–8)

There is an ascent out of the depths of your secret escape. You can't do it by yourself. Accountability to others can help, but it won't reach down into the abyss of your sin and bring you out. For every trap of secret escape there is only one path to freedom. It is blazed by the steadfast love of the Lord. It is this steadfast love that sent the Son of God into the world to purchase sinners for God. The steadfast love of the Lord put Jesus on the cross so that his blood would ransom you from your sin and set you free from the trap of secret escape.

Is it enough? Is the steadfast love of the Lord enough to set you free? The psalmist leaves no doubt. It is a plentiful redemption. I love the way older translations say it—"plenteous redemption." Plenteous redemption is abundant, overflowing redemption. Lasting redemption, redemption that fills in the cracks of our unbelief and lifts us out of our cravings. It is there with us in every temptation and at every moment of temptation. With us, there is hiding and plentiful sin. With God, there is steadfast love and plenteous redemption. There is no millisecond when you are considering your secret escape that there isn't plenteous redemption providing the way to freedom.

This psalm ends in an amazing place. "O Israel, hope in the LORD!" The writer who began in the depths of sin and separation from God is calling others to hope in the Lord. Can you imagine doing this? Maybe you should try. Maybe your hopes have been set too low. Is it enough to be able to look in a mirror without self-recrimination? To sit in a hotel room by yourself and not know it is just a matter of time before you give in to temptation? You would love to go to the beach and not see people through eyes of envy or lust. But redemption is more than not being trapped. It is being free. Believe that a day is coming when you will be able to declare the redemption of God in your life to others. Your story is more than survival. It is a redemption story being written in spite of pain, tears, regrets, and failures along the way. Someday you'll be able to share it with others who are trapped and need to know the way out.

Can you sing this song of ascent? Perhaps even after considering this you're thinking, *That's great for some, but I've begged God to get me out of this, and it just hasn't worked. Maybe I'm just beyond redeeming.*

If that's where you're tempted to go, consider this. Jesus didn't come to save normal people but avoid people like you. People like you are the reason he came. Gospel writer Luke makes this abundantly clear as he shows us how Jesus defined his own ministry. Jesus's first public act recorded in Luke is when he teaches in the Nazareth synagogue. Here's the way Luke describes it:

> And the scroll of the prophet Isaiah was given to him. He unrolled the scroll and found the place where it was written,
>   "The Spirit of the Lord is upon me,
>   because he has anointed me
>   to proclaim good news to the poor.
> He has sent me to proclaim liberty to the captives
>   and recovering of sight to the blind,
>   to set at liberty those who are oppressed,
>   to proclaim the year of the Lord's favor."
> And he rolled up the scroll and gave it back to the attendant and sat down. And the eyes of all in the synagogue were fixed on him. And he began to say to them, "Today this Scripture has been fulfilled in your hearing." (Luke 4:17–21)

What's astounding to his listeners is how Jesus applies this magnificent Messianic prophecy to himself. What is equally astounding to you and me is that we are included in his words as well. Are you poor and destitute in your secret trap? The good news of Jesus is for you. Are you held captive by your destructive fixations? Jesus has proclaimed liberty over you. Have you lost sight of the good in life? Jesus will give you fresh vision. Are you oppressed by your sin? The liberty of gracious redemption is yours.

Do you know what is *not* yours? It is what Jesus left out of his reading. He finishes his reading from Isaiah with the first half of Isaiah 61:2: "to proclaim the year of the LORD's favor."

He closes the scroll before reading what comes next: "the day of vengeance of our God" (Isaiah 61:2b).

There will be a day of vengeance, but if you have looked to Jesus, then that day is not your day. Your day is the day of favor. Trust Jesus to free you from your poverty, your prison, your blindness, your oppression. Ask him to make this a daily reality in your life. Hope in God. This is the year of God's favor for all who are trapped in secret escape. It is the year of steadfast love. It is the year of plentiful redemption. Let this be your song of ascent.

Chapter 8

THE ADDICTIONS TRAP

Ann is a heartbroken mom. Her little girl, who used to make up songs for her stuffed animals, who danced at recitals, who showed so much promise as a teenager, is going back to jail. The eyes that used to sparkle are now hard and vacant. Lorraine used to write stories; now she just spins out lies and deception. Trust is gone. The family pictures on the walls mockingly remind everyone of what has been lost. How did we get here?

The addictions trap. Lorraine has fallen into it and has taken her future and her loved ones into it with her. An entire family is chained to one sad individual who lives only for the intense, immediate impact of chemicals pushing dopamine through her brain. In Lorraine's world, it is called getting high, but in Lorraine's prison of addiction and abuse, there is no longer anything high about it. Drugs don't bring pleasure; they just temporarily dull the cruel slave-masters of physical craving and self-loathing.

Addiction has been called many things in our culture. An epidemic. A curse. A war. A moral evil. A social blight. A criminal economy. It is all those things. But if you struggle with addictions, the trap is personal and intense. You may get some relief and even some temporary reprieve, but you know the tyrant is lurking in the shadows. Today's clean can't wash away yesterday's filth, and it doesn't guarantee freedom for tomorrow.

The addictions trap is maddeningly convoluted. Some of the most problematic addictive agents, like nicotine and alcohol, are abundantly available and culturally accepted, if not exalted. Those addictions that we sometimes call "hard core"— think needles, crime, crack houses, emaciated bodies, and celebrity overdoses—seem like obvious traps to those of us on the outside. But they are life, purpose, and meaning to those who are caught in them. That's why rehab centers and support groups are filled with people who aren't there by choice, but by consequence or judicial requirement.

About nine years after his tragic death from suicide, the personal reflections of Nirvana's Kurt Cobain were published as *Journals* (2003). Within the raw pages of his private notes, the artist opened a searingly ambivalent window into the hold and the horror of addiction. Cobain said he began to use heroin as a way to anesthetize untreatable stomach pain. His addictions trap was not simply a drug habit, it was a chaotic lifestyle fed by a need for physical relief, overwhelming pressure from the expectations of others, a history of emotional turmoil, and traveling in a world where drugs were readily available and abuse almost expected. In an interview, the artist alluded to the dead-end life that comes with addiction.

I just thought it was one of those things you do to relieve the pain. But as I expected, before I started doing heroin . . . I knew at the beginning that it would become just as boring as marijuana does, you know. Like all drugs, after a few months it's just as boring as breathing air. . . . I've always lied about it because I don't want anyone to consider using drugs. It's just stupid.[1]

Cobain was never able to translate his disdain for drugs into freedom. His tragic life and haunting words speak to some hard realities about any kind of addiction. You hear in his words the sober reflections of someone who sought escape in something that took pain away for a brief time, but exacted a terrible price in the process. In the end there is no sustaining drive to escape the trap, only resignation that he is caught. It isn't that people battling addiction don't care anymore. There is always a flesh-and-blood person in the trap, and you'll hear the beleaguered voice trying to find a reason to fight a way out. As one woman posted on the web, "I can't stand the confusion. My whole life has turned into one big 'why' . . . My life's dream has become to find out what makes this uncontrollable engine run, and how to stop it."

TOURING THE ADDICTIONS TRAP

What does Lorraine know about addictions? She knows a lot.

Lorraine would have been told by her school that addictions are a threat. Her health class would provide ample statistics meant to drive her away from temptation. She would be told to choose her social world carefully and stay in school. She would have told herself that drugs are stupid and that she would never be addicted to anything.

Lorraine would have been told by friends that drugs are just a thing to do, that drinking was cool, that cutting was honest, that sex was fun. You just do it and don't think about it. She would have told herself that one time wouldn't matter; she was strong and could handle it. Lorraine would have told herself that it felt good to drink or smoke or cut or hook up. She would listen to music and watch things that celebrated the rightness of what she was doing. Lorraine would fall in with people who liked feeling the way she felt. They would help each other get the good feeling. Maybe the feeling was pleasure; maybe it was the dulling of emotional pain. Lorraine would tell herself, why shouldn't I do what feels good?

Lorraine would have been told by her body that she needed it, that to go without was impossible, that she needed her drug of choice to survive. Not even mounting consequences would dull the drive. Lorraine started telling herself that nothing mattered but feeding the need.

Lorraine would have been told by her family that she was bad. Maybe not in so many words, but she would feel like the black sheep. When you lie and steal and manipulate the people you love, you are a pretty bad person. Nobody in the family could convince her otherwise, because deep down that's the way they felt.

Lorraine would have been told by the courts that she was a criminal, that people like her were a plague on society, and that if she didn't get straight, she didn't deserve to live a free life. She would have a hard time arguing with that verdict.

Lorraine would have been told in rehab that she had a disease. That her own body was at fault and that she was a victim of radical changes in the way her brain worked. That would explain how hard it was to change, but it wouldn't explain all the other things she had been told.

WHAT IS ADDICTION?

The short definition of addiction provided by The American Society of Addiction Medicine (ASAM) is:

> Addiction is a primary, chronic disease of brain reward, motivation, memory and related circuitry. Dysfunction in these circuits leads to characteristic biological, psychological, social and spiritual manifestations. This is reflected in an individual pathologically pursuing reward and/or relief by substance use and other behaviors.[2]

This definition, which is fairly typical of current terminology, does one thing well and one thing poorly. What it does well is highlight the complex ways addiction interacts with life. What it does poorly is help someone like Lorraine. It tells her that her addiction is in her brain. But that confuses her. It seems to say that she's not a person; she is just a malfunctioning biological machine that needs to be rewired for optimal productivity. This is confusing to her because she knows the physical craving for the drugs, and she also knows the moral choices she makes to get them.

There is, however, a different way of thinking about addictions that speaks to all the ways Lorraine has experienced her struggles in life. It is found in the Bible. This way of seeing addictions is rooted in an understanding of who Lorraine is, not just as an addict, but as a person who has been created in the image of God to live for his glory. The Word of God will lead us to see addictions as a form of false worship, of idol worship. In his excellent resource *Addictions: A Banquet in the Grave*, neuropsychologist and counselor Ed Welch would define Lorraine's condition this way:

> Addiction is bondage to the rule of a substance, activity, or state of mind, which then becomes the center of life, defending itself from the truth so that even bad consequences don't bring repentance, and leading to further estrangement from God.[3]

In other words, an addiction is a full-bodied worship of an idol of your own choosing that now controls and defines you.

There is nothing unbiblical about acknowledging the physiology of addictions. The fact that dopamine release to the pleasure centers of the brain can be identified as the place where addictions play their chemical games simply speaks to the physicality of our addictions, not the cause. There is nothing unbiblical about acknowledging that some people are more genetically predisposed to addiction than others. Genetic factors speak to a tendency, not a causality. There is nothing unbiblical about acknowledging the socioeconomic, environmental, and cultural factors that influence addiction. In fact, a biblical understanding of sin is ultimately the only causality that encompasses all these other factors. And it adds one most important additional factor: Our addictions are false worship to enslaving gods.

I want to be careful here. When religiously-oriented people see biological terms like "disease" in a definition of addictions, they think that this means "medical," like cancer or heart disease. The latter diseases can be identified in a laboratory, and some treatment regimen can specifically target, if not cure, the pathological condition. Religious people see the foolishness of addiction and the immoral behavior that surrounds it. They can feel that talking about it in terms of biology is a cop-out. If you're a religious person, please don't shut me down here.

I want to make the same appeal to people who see addictions primarily as disease. When scientifically-oriented people hear the word "worship," what comes to mind is a spiritual belief with no basis in hard evidence, along with moral laws that flow out of that non-rational belief. This comment by a prominent researcher typifies this dismissive perspective: "Alcohol- and substance-use disorders are the realm of medicine. This is not the realm of priests."[4]

Unfortunately, this talking past each other between the medical and spiritual communities leaves a gaping hole in treatment and understanding, through which many people struggling with addictions fall. Many faith-based approaches oversimplify the moral will to change. They are rightly critiqued for the implied message that those who don't kick addictions just don't want to. Many medical approaches oversimplify the effectiveness of drugs to battle drugs. In reality, most "medical" treatment plans for addictions require a substantial amount of personal commitment by the addicted person to be effective.

Here's my contention. The Bible offers the clearest, deepest, and most comprehensive diagnosis of the human condition that we will ever encounter in this life. And the gospel of redemption is the only treatment that brings the power, change, and hope that can transform broken addicts into whole-hearted worshippers of God. A reasoned biblical approach will make a place for the biological without deifying it. If you are skeptical of this assertion and don't buy my premise, just keep reading. I'm going to work from one concise but compelling passage of Scripture. My intent is not to reduce all that can be biblically said about addictions to a few verses. And I certainly wouldn't want anyone to think that if they can just "get" this, they will be done with their addiction. No, what I want to offer is a blueprint for understanding the pathway to freedom that you can walk over time. If you can see the road, you'll be able to see your progress, your ruts, your detours, your blind spots, your obstacles, and your help along the way.

A PATH OUT OF THE ADDICTIONS TRAP

The passage we'll look at is from the apostle Paul's letter to Titus, a pastor he has trained and whom he is now advising. The short letter concerns a group of people who have expressed belief in Christ and are being brought together to form a church on the island of Crete. "Cretans" (from the island of Crete) apparently had a well-earned reputation as "liars, evil beasts, lazy gluttons" (Titus 1:12). Substance abuse seems to have been a big part of the problem. Titus was to exhort even the best of the men toward sobriety (implying that they weren't always that way), and strikingly, to urge women to stop being slaves (literally addicted) to excessive drinking as well (Titus 2:2–6). It's almost as if this is a recovery group that needs to become a church of productive, maturing disciples. At the center of this letter, Paul lays out the gospel treatment plan.

For the grace of God has appeared, bringing salvation for all people, training us to renounce ungodliness and worldly passions, and to live self-controlled, upright, and godly lives in the present age, waiting for our blessed hope, the appearing of the glory of our great God and Savior Jesus Christ, who gave himself for us to redeem us from all lawlessness and to purify for himself a people for his own possession who are zealous for good works. (Titus 2:11–14)

Let's walk through this plan step by step and find the hope and power for freedom from addictions.

"FOR THE GRACE OF GOD HAS APPEARED, BRINGING SALVATION FOR ALL PEOPLE" (V. 11)

The road to freedom begins with acknowledging what every person in addiction feels—the sense of powerlessness to overcome the addiction. This is the experiential reality that flows out of addiction—I'm trapped in something and I can't get myself out. The biological approach offers the very helpful diagnostic that this is the message you are getting from your body. The pleasure centers of the brain react and adapt to the chemicals you ingest. Brain scans show that repetitive behaviors and thought patterns have the same addictive effect over time. So telling an addicted person (like Lorraine) "Don't do it" is to sentence her to repeated failures of self-attempt. "Guilting" people to change just produces more guilt. The sheer effort to try to change your brain through will power is beyond the resolve of most people. As one person confessed, "The shame and guilt, coupled with the fear of having to withstand the pain of withdrawal, sapped what little resolve I had left to reach out for help."[5]

Freedom from addiction can't come through our own efforts to escape. The Twelve Step programs have always known this. The first three steps of Alcoholics Anonymous speak of powerlessness over the struggle, the need for a higher power, and a commitment to turn over the struggle to that higher power. Whether you're trying desperately to align yourself with the agenda of "god as you understand him/her/it," or finding yourself in the maze of clinics, therapists, and insurance carriers that direct your medical treatment, what Paul says here is a total game-changer. Paul not only declares that we need that power outside us, but he says that it has already come to us in the grace of Jesus Christ! When we read "the grace of God has appeared," what we're meant to see is literally an epiphany of grace. That's the word Paul is using. An epiphany is a breaking in of light into darkness. As one commentator says, grace is "the great penetrator, dispelling the darkness for all and bringing salvation to all."[6] That epiphany of grace isn't something you go looking for. It entered your world first in the incarnation of Jesus Christ over two thousand years ago (John 1:5, 14, 16; John 8:12).

If you are caught in the trap of addictions, know that the One who brings grace has come and he takes note of you. He does not stand over you as a judge. He is your Redeemer. We don't seek him, but he sought us, and you will have to seek out new darkness to avoid him. Grace is here to bring you into the freedom of God's loving ownership, care, and protection. As Ed Welch says, "The grace of God is what God has done and what he is presently doing. He has sent Jesus to liberate us from the harsh bondage of our own desires."[7]

The good news for Lorraine is that this liberating salvation is offered to all people. She is not too far gone for grace. She may have messed up a lot, but she can't mess up grace. It is irresistible and indomitable. Maybe you're reading this and you can't point to substance abuse. Your addiction has been to gambling, or food, or sex, or to any of a host of experiences or sensations that humans turn into functional gods. Maybe you feel that extra bit of shame that there isn't some outside agent that has messed with your dopamine flow. You've done it all through stupid self-will. But now you're trapped. The good news to you is that grace does not rank or rate addictions. You are among the "all" to whom grace has appeared. Regardless of your bondage of choice, receive grace and begin to see the dawning of your freedom.

". . . TRAINING US TO RENOUNCE UNGODLINESS AND WORLDLY PASSIONS" (V. 12A)

Churches love to have "victorious" addicts give testimonies in meetings. Nothing shows us the power of grace like someone who was bound in addiction telling the story of how grace broke into his or her life. I believe these stories to be genuine and sincere, but I think we sometimes celebrate the dawning of grace like it's the finished work of grace. Well-meaning Christians rightly celebrate the appearance of grace, but their enthusiasm can sometimes lead a sincere new convert to think that a new sense of freedom is all that grace is about. That's not

Paul's perspective. The grace that breaks in has a job to do. Paul uses the culturally familiar metaphor of pedagogy (teaching) to describe what grace is intending to do.

Grace comes to Lorraine and sees layers of guilt and shame. Maybe she can grasp that God has forgiven her of her sin, but she can't look her family in the eye. Beneath that is a self-loathing Lorraine can't even describe. She remembers back when she swore she would never do the things her addiction led her to do, but here she is. She knows each step of compromise and rationalization that took her into the addictions trap. Well-meaning counselors might work hard to keep her from focusing on her moral duplicity, but grace asks the honest questions, the essential questions. Where did you get your self-confidence in the first place? What made you think you were better or stronger than others? You see, grace identifies the self-worship in self-condemnation. Grace is after the things that led her into addictive behavior before her brain ever had the chance to adapt to it.

Grace is going to help Lorraine say no to ungodliness, that condition where our false worship develops into a lifestyle of sinful choices. Lorraine is going to learn the value of a repentant life. Repentance is not self-atonement. Lorraine can't pay her way out of bondage. The ransom has been paid for her by Christ on the cross. But even before she can regularly say No to the powerful urges of her addiction, she can begin to say No to worldly passions—the familiar props of her addictive lifestyle. She can cut off associations that have proven destructive to her life. She can change secondary patterns that feed the addiction, like the media she imbibes and the self-absorption that sets her up as needy and misunderstood. She can begin to address habits of lying and deception that keep help at a distance. Grace motivates you to say No where No needs to be said.

. . . AND TO LIVE SELF-CONTROLLED, UPRIGHT, AND GODLY LIVES IN THE PRESENT AGE (V. 12B)

If No was all the Bible offered, then change would be a tough row to hoe. But grace the teacher has more Yes than No in its curriculum. What is desperately needed is a new, non-addictive way of life, and that is what grace training is all about. First is the Yes of a self-controlled life. The Greek word translated "self-controlled" may be accurately translated "sober." So sobriety is essential to that new life. Sobriety isn't the same as abstinence (total non-exposure), though abstinence may be important for many people as they seek to say No to their drug of choice. But the long-term Yes is not to abstinence, it is to sobriety. Sobriety is the appropriate and balanced use of anything in this world that might bring pleasure or enjoyment in a way that doesn't violate God's commands or our conscience, lead us into false worship, or lead others to stumble. Sobriety replaces a fear of failure with wisdom for ourselves and love for others. It lines up with the larger goals grace has for us in life.

Second is the Yes of uprightness. To live "upright" in this world speaks to life in relationship to other people. To be upright is not to be self-right. One struggle recovering addicts have is that they tend to relate only to others who have been in addictions. They don't identify with non-addicts, and they don't think non-addicts can understand them. Recovery groups can be a crucial refuge for a person seeking to get free from addictions. Addictions groups can have an important function in helping people talk through their struggles in an understanding and supportive environment. But some folks treat what should be a transition in recovery groups into a retreat from relationships where addiction isn't a familiar reference point.

Grace doesn't leave people in recovery. Grace pushes us into the world where we see that addictions aren't the only traps that bind people. Lorraine needs to see that there is other suffering in the world beyond her addictions suffering. She needs to learn to talk about her life in a way that doesn't require a fellow addict to understand and help her. She needs to learn sympathy, and not disdain the trials and temptations of non-addicts. Uprightness by grace discovers that we all need redemption and rejoices whenever we see it in others.

Third is the Yes of godliness. Godly living is not perfect living. It is a daily life of hearing and obeying God's Word. People in addictions are used to self-deception, hypocrisy, and doing whatever it takes to get what you want. Grace reorients people away from fleshly, dopamine-craving habits to heart-located, grace-motivated habits. The Bible calls this sanctification—the progressive heart transformation that is displayed in a transformed life.

But often the physiological compulsions of deep addiction and the self-destructive spiral that results need to be addressed in proactive ways. Here is where I think we can see a role for rightly-administered medications. The disorder in the thoughts and feelings of a person who has been addicted for an extended time can make clear thinking and impulse control very difficult. Addictions may also mix with manic or depressive tendencies or mood volatility in a way that severely impairs a person's ability to make consistent, rational, self-denying choices. Pharmacology may moderate and even correct some of the brain chemistry issues present with addictions. It is not *the* answer because medicine alone can never produce godliness. Godliness addresses flesh and heart, sin and weakness, thoughts and behaviors, choices and circumstances as present-day realities in need of grace. The training agenda is a "self-controlled, upright, and godly life in this present age"—in other words, living as a day-to-day God-worshipper in the fallen world we all inhabit.

". . . WAITING FOR OUR BLESSED HOPE, THE APPEARING OF THE GLORY OF OUR GREAT GOD AND SAVIOR JESUS CHRIST . . ." (V. 13)

One of the hardest things for a person coming out of addictions to do is to wait. Addiction is the opposite of waiting. It is the subordination of everything else in life to the immediate gratification of the one thing the addiction craves. But life isn't about instant relief and immediate satisfaction. So grace takes up this compulsivity and tells us to learn to wait. Then it teaches the joy in waiting. The word translated "wait" isn't about just doing without. It is a joyful anticipation of something better to come. Addiction produces intense immediate sensations, but there is no joy. Joy isn't a God-high. Joy is its own thing, to be valued for its own right.

This joy is forward-looking. It is looking for the next great epiphany, the appearing of our great God and Savior Jesus Christ at the culmination of all things. This is a life-sustaining, hope-inspiring, trial-transcending expectancy that the Savior who came into the world to free us from sin will come again to bring us to the Promised Land of heaven. In this land there will be no pain needing medication, no thrill needing to be satisfied, no high needing to be reached. Joy can't be manufactured, smoked, snorted, injected, served on the rocks, dispensed from a tap, won at the tables, picked up at a club, ingested with a spoon, or consumed on the web. It comes as a precious anticipatory grace with eternal blessing in Christ as its fulfillment. It is worth the wait.

... WHO GAVE HIMSELF FOR US TO REDEEM US FROM ALL LAWLESSNESS AND TO PURIFY FOR HIMSELF A PEOPLE FOR HIS OWN POSSESSION WHO ARE ZEALOUS FOR GOOD WORKS (V. 14)

As I've talked through this issue, I hope you can see my respect for the physiological aspects of addictions. But there is one area where I believe that the biological model, no matter how evidence-based it is, misses the issue. And misses it badly. That is in the area of guilt. The following quote is typical of what you will find in much of the biological-model addictions material:

> Don't blame yourself! Recovery is much easier when you feel good about yourself and refrain from seeing yourself as bad, worthless, or wrong. No one chooses to get trapped in a destructive lifestyle of drug use—and you are not to blame for trying to make yourself feel better in the one way you found that worked.[8]

Statements like this are meant to be compassionate and to speak to the self-condemnation that is part and parcel with addictions. But I've never met anyone struggling with addictions who found this ultimately helpful. Because at a functional level, everyone who has lived with addictions feels guilty and can point to the wrong they have done. To muffle guilt and shame with self-esteem simply doesn't speak in a meaningful way to the complex personal and relational damage that addiction has done. The real truth, the liberating truth, begins with acknowledging a guilt that goes deeper and binds us more strongly than any addiction. The bondage of sin is the root of addiction; it is also what the addict shares with everyone else. At the core of our addictive nature, we don't need medical intervention, dopamine rerouting, talk therapy, behavior modification, or detox. We need redemption.

Are you picking up on some themes in Paul's language that we've seen earlier in this book? John Stott's commentary on this passage ties it together.

> Paul deliberately chooses Old Testament words and images from the beginnings of Israel as a nation, so as to portray Christ's salvation as the fulfilment of these foreshadowings. Thus "gave himself for us" ("sacrificed himself for us") recalls the Passover sacrifice; "to redeem us" the exodus redemption from Egyptian bondage; and "a people that are his very own" the Sinaitic covenant by which Israel became Yahweh's "treasured possession." Paul uses the very expression *laos periousios* ("chosen people") which [The Septuagint] uses. Thus we enjoy a direct continuity with the Old Testament people of God, for we are his redeemed people and he is our Passover, our exodus and our Sinai.[9]

Paul's instructions here connect us backward to the great truth that we have been purchased out of bondage into freedom under the loving ownership of God. They also point us forward to the reality of an eternal destiny that belongs to us in Christ. Addicts need to locate themselves on this spiritual journey, to see themselves on pilgrimage to the Promised Land. That keeps the big picture of life in view and connects them to the great journey that all of God's people are walking together.

If you have been trapped in addictions, don't settle for abstinence or for medically curbed addictive drives. Your Redeemer has a greater goal in mind. He has ransomed you out of the addictions trap to live in this world as a blessing, not a curse. He has good works for you to do—works that will make an eternal difference in the lives of others. You are more than an addict, more than your recovery lifestyle. Regardless of how you're doing today, your road of freedom out of addiction is a path led and empowered by grace. There is a place for you among the ransomed and redeemed.

Chapter 9

TRAPPED IN A TROUBLED MARRIAGE

Before we revisit Michael and Tina's marriage, let's take a little imaginary journey with yours.

Imagine you and your spouse have taken to spelunking—cave exploration. You stopped at the hiking store and looked at all the spelunking gear they recommend. "Do we need all this? We're taking a stroll into a cave and then coming back out. How complicated can that be?" You get a lamp and some water bottles and embark on the adventure. The cave seems friendly enough—an inviting entrance, even a place to take pictures. As you take your first steps, the path is wide and smooth. The bright afternoon sun is shining into the cave, illuminating the beautiful rock formations you have come to explore. As you move farther in, the sunlight recedes and your eyes are having a more difficult time adjusting to the encroaching darkness. But you have your lamp and it is just enough illumination to see the path and the walls of the narrowing cavern. There is a growing sense of uncertainty that you both begin to feel. You're together on the path but alone in an unfamiliar world.

At some point, the thrill of spelunking begins to give way to the relentless darkness and a foreboding realization that you are deeper into this than you ever thought you'd be. As you look at each other in the yellow illumination of the lantern, it's hard to recognize the person standing next to you. In the darkness you feel like strangers. You turn together and look for the way back, but there is no clear passage, just a series of rocky paths. How did we get here? Now we're trapped. How do we get out?

This is where we find Michael and Tina from chapter 1. Except they're not trapped in a cave; they're trapped in a marriage. A marriage they willingly entered into and inhabited for several years. But it isn't what they thought it would be at the beginning. Michael and Tina both seem mystified as to how they got lost along the way.

Something that seemed so right at the wedding has turned out so wrong. The person who seemed like a perfect partner at the outset is now almost unrecognizable in the flickering light of misunderstandings and unmet expectations. Michael and Tina are trapped in a troubled marriage and they don't know how to get out of it. The sense of darkness plays tricks with what they see. Each feels like the other is the main reason they are trapped. They see each other's faults in glaring clarity. But they can't seem to see what the other person sees; they can't see their own contribution to the trouble. It may be that the problems originate more with one partner than the other, but even an innocent party in a troubled marriage is living in the troubles. No matter how we get stuck, every marriage trap has two people in it.

IS THERE ANY WAY OUT?

The two lost spelunkers in our imaginary excursion do agree on one thing: they can't stay where they are. Looking around, they can see multiple pathways to take. From where they stand, they all look the same, but only one is the way out. The others could lead anywhere or nowhere. That's the challenge that people in troubled marriages face. It's a sober recognition that things have to change, but with no clear direction on where to go next. Sadly, for desperate people in troubled marriages one direction that seems most inviting is the escape of divorce or separation. Let me address each of these potential paths head-on.

DIVORCE

The remedy that is generally offered to people who are trapped in a relationship is to simply break free—to get out while you can. There was a time when societal conventions kept people from fleeing unhappy marriages through the path of divorce. But that isn't the case anymore. Marriage is just a more legally and economically complicated trap than other arrangements, but there are escape plans for it. If you are counseling people who feel trapped in a marriage, you can be sure that someone is encouraging them to get out of the marriage some way, somehow. We can be sure that, somewhere in their thinking, the option of divorce has occurred to Michael and Tina.

Having read this book, you can probably anticipate that I'm not going to recommend divorce as an escape from a troubled marriage. It will probably serve you best for me to be clear on my stand regarding divorce, based on my understanding of the

Scriptures. Marriage is a gift from God that can be enjoyed by believers and unbelievers alike. It is defined by a lifelong covenant union between a man and a woman, entered into for the purpose of companionship, sexual intimacy, procreation (Genesis 2:20–25) and, most deeply, to radiate the love Christ has for his church (Ephesians 5:22–31). Because marriage has been established by God, it is to be held in the highest regard and honored by all (Hebrews 13:4). The Scriptures permit divorce only when a spouse commits sins that involve sexual immorality (Matthew 19:3–9) or when an unbelieving spouse abandons a marriage (1 Corinthians 7:10–16). It is important to note that, although God permits divorce in such cases, divorce is not required. In fact, seeking repentance and reconciliation should always be the first recourse.

That's my position, but I don't live looking for opportunities to impose or defend it. When I encounter people who are considering divorce, what flows up in my heart is sadness and mercy. I'm sad because no one gets married looking forward to divorce. It is an excruciating, shame-inducing, life-hammering, world-shattering admission of failure. It isn't always personal failure, because people in divorces can often be the victims of a spouse's abuse of the marriage covenant. But even victims of divorce feel failure in the breakup of a marriage. My heart breaks for those whose lives are torn by divorce, no matter how it came to pass. Tim Keller's words reflect the grace and truth balance I want to have when dealing with people considering escape from a troubled marriage through divorce.

Wedding vows are not a declaration of present love but a mutually binding promise of future love. A wedding should not be primarily a celebration of how loving you feel now—that can safely be assumed. Rather, in a wedding you stand up before God, your family, and all the main institutions of society, and you promise to be loving, faithful, and true to the other person in the future, regardless of undulating internal feelings or external circumstances. . . . To allow divorce for almost any reason is to hollow out the very concept of covenant and vow. Divorce should not be easy; it should not be our first, second, third, or fourth resort.[1]

The divorce path can seem an inviting path of "first resort" for someone trying to escape a troubled marriage, but it is rarely a clean break into daylight. It is a wise and loving God who protects marriages through his Word from the powerful but deceptive attraction of escape through divorce.

SEPARATION

Michael and Tina may be thinking, *I just need a break from this. If I could just get away from it, maybe I could figure out what to do.* Most people who say they want out of trapped marriages really just want some kind of relief from their present experience. That's why the idea of separation can be so attractive. But most separations only bring temporary relief and they never bring freedom. Separation usually just exchanges the trap of a troubled marriage for the trap of an undefined temporary reprieve.

Separation as a route out of a troubled marriage is rarely a clear or well-lit path. There are biblical considerations (1

Corinthians 7:1–5, for example, calls for separations to be short if they happen at all), as well as legal ramifications and logistical concerns that cannot be ignored. But let me say this about separation as an escape from a troubled marriage: it usually isn't. It can be a respite from constant strife, a refuge from an unstable or abusive situation, or a strategic means of addressing the practical problems that need to be addressed for a marriage to be reconciled. But a separation is by definition temporary; therefore, it needs a plan so that it is not simply an avoidance of problems. Separation usually requires the thoughtful agreement of both parties, not just the desires of one. Most people seeking a separation are doing it unilaterally, with no plan beyond getting out of a perceived trap. Ill-considered separations typically prolong and complicate the troubles in a marriage. Separation will affect your experience of the trap, but will not spring you from it.

The good news is that you can get free from the trap of a troubled marriage without divorce or separation. The greatest hope for a troubled marriage is not its end but its transformation. For that to happen, you need to come to terms with how your marriage became a trap and how your identity as God's redeemed servants can empower you to climb out of the darkness into which you have stumbled.

HOW DID WE GET INTO THIS TRAP?

What we want from marriage as we go into it can be part of the trap. A person coming from a home where there has been divorce or serious marital dysfunction will often see marriage much differently than someone whose family upbringing was more stable or conventional. A couple who has been living together and decides to tie the knot will approach marriage in a whole different frame of mind than two young people who have been living at home with family prior to a wedding. And men and women can enter marriage with wildly different perspectives. Consequently, some don't discover that marriage is a trap until they get into it. Often the way to freedom from the marriage trap requires us to retrace the steps we've taken. In my pastoral experience, I have seen three ways that marriage becomes a trap.

Poor Preparation

It has been said quite accurately that people prepare much more thoroughly for a driver's license than a marriage license. I'm glad that it takes preparation to get a driver's license, but it is a fact that most couples get married with little thoughtful preparation for the lifetime commitment they are making. For most people, an engagement has nothing to do with preparing for marriage and everything do to with planning a wedding—usually a big event—and a new lifestyle.

Perhaps you have come to the realization that you didn't give sufficient thought to what you were looking for in marriage before the wedding. Or maybe you lived together prior to marriage and you thought that the wedding was more of a ceremony than a significant change in your life together. People use marriage as an escape from aloneness, as a hope for security, as a means to have a family, as a way to prove to others that they are adults. All of these things can happen with marriage, but none is a reason to get married. And if they are made the reason to get married, then marriage can become a trap very early on.

If you feel trapped in a troubled marriage, please consider whether a lack of preparation is part of the problem. I've seen couples find great reasons to rebuild their marriage when they discover that current problems have roots that can be addressed with humility, honest communication, and a willingness to tear down familiar things and build up new things.

Unexpected Turns

Even marriages with a sound foundation can become troubled. Life is hard. We do the best we can, but trials and unexpected turns can take a toll on relationships even where the love is deep and the commitment sound. Unexpected financial struggles, job losses, chronic or debilitating illness, struggles with children and parenting, infertility, moral failures, unintended consequences of well-meant decisions can all send marriages into dark places, far beyond anything the couple expected. Sometimes the turns can be overcome, or at least endured until they end. But sometimes these turns become part of life. The sense that "I didn't sign up for this" can be overwhelming. That other person who was going to be your rock begins to crumble, and you don't have strength for yourself, let alone for him or her. There's nobody to blame, but everything feels wrong. The small cracks that are in every marriage get exposed to unbearable pressure and even good marriages can start to feel like traps. If you haven't faced this, you certainly know someone who has.

Careless Wandering

Michael and Tina talk about the way things were when they first got married. It seems so different now, but neither can point to a moment or event that changed things. Marriages can become traps little by little over time. It usually isn't a dramatic change. My guess is that every marriage, to some extent at some point in time, can feel like a bit of a trap. No spouse is such a soul mate that you don't wonder at times why, after all these years, you can feel so misunderstood. Busyness and parenting and the stuff of life can lead us to think that a well-functioning domestic environment is the same as a thriving marriage. We can get careless about appreciating each other, content with conflict avoidance or non-resolution, thoughtless with our words. These are wanderings that lead to a sense of isolation and regret in marriage, the loss of what you have always considered the most important thing in your life. Marriage therapists often talk about "drift," the experience of a marriage without a sense of purpose and direction. The end result of uninterrupted drift can be the trap of isolation and regret. Even good marriages can wander into bad traps.

Please hear my pastoral heart at this point. The last thing I want to do when I'm sitting with a couple trapped in a troubled marriage is to walk them through a list of things they may have done wrong. In fact, I deliberately don't start there. But who will raise the question? The tendency of most couples in marriage counseling is to focus so exclusively on the problems that they don't consider how they got *into* the problems. There is an underlying fear that if they look at how they got into the trap, they'll just fall further into the abyss. But giving serious thought to how your marriage turned into a trap will actually position you to see the redeeming light of God in the darkness.

REDEEMER AND RESCUER

No matter how trapped you may feel in your marriage, no matter how confusing and suffocating the dark cavern of disappointment may be, Jesus the Redeemer knows where you are. He didn't lose sight of the Israelites trapped in slavery in Egypt. He doesn't lose track of lost and broken people trapped in the bondage of sin. And he does not lose track of people in even the bleakest marriages. He has his eye on you and on your spouse. And he is about the work of redemption in your marriage. How do you know? Because marriage, according to the Bible, belongs to God.

This is really good news for troubled marriages. If your marriage belongs to you, then you will live in the suffocating hole of responsibility for something you can't fix on your own. If your marriage belongs to your spouse, then he or she becomes the ball and chain that keeps you from where you want to go with your life. If a marriage belongs to a couple, or to the kids, or to a religious tradition, or to the dictates of social custom, then you find yourself where our disoriented spelunkers found themselves—lost in confusion with no clear direction forward.

Michael and Tina would both say they want God's help for their marriage. But what they mean is that they want God to do something in the other person to resolve the problems. They aren't really looking for God to change them so that they can live out what God designed marriage to be. That's why nothing seems to be helping. They can't get traction because they don't know where they are going. But if marriage belongs to God, then he has a plan of rescue and a goal you can pursue. That makes all the difference in a troubled marriage.

God's plan and goal for redeeming marriage is found in the Bible. To properly understand and apply biblical texts on marriage to our troubled relationships, we need to read them in context. It can be unhelpful to pick marriage verses out of the Bible and paste them onto our circumstances. We need to read these passages in light of the people and situations they are initially addressing. We need to consider the literary context—why the writer is addressing the issue of marriage at that point in his discourse. There is always a bigger picture in mind when the Bible addresses marriage. Marriage texts in the Bible are never just about marriage. They are first about the God who created marriage, who designed it for his good purposes, and who blesses or frustrates our use of marriage based on his larger redemptive purposes for the people he has purchased for his glory.

Let me offer some resources to help you get the big picture of marriage. For an excellent perspective on what the whole Bible has to say about marriage and the family, I would recommend that you read *God, Marriage, and Family* by Andreas J. Kostenberger. For a culturally nuanced treatment of the biblical vision for marriage, I encourage you to read Tim Keller's *The Meaning of Marriage* (from which I've quoted above). And for an excellent pastoral application of the gospel to marriage problems, I would encourage you to read *What Did You Expect?* by Paul David Tripp. Knowing these excellent resources are available for you to study, I'm going to restrict my focus to one passage on marriage.

THE TOUGH FREEDOM OF 1 PETER 2:4—3:7

Please take a few minutes to read 1 Peter 2:4—3:7. It is a lengthy passage that ends with some very specific direction on marriage. Why focus on these words from Peter? Two primary reasons. One is that Peter's instruction on marriage in 1 Peter 3:1–7 is specifically addressing troubled marriages. Peter's words are directed to believers in a region newly impacted by the gospel. One result is that married women are coming to faith in Jesus. They are trying to determine how to live as followers of Christ in marriages to unbelieving husbands who oppose their newfound faith. And this means trouble.

A larger reason to focus on this passage is that Peter's words on marriage flow out of a deep concern for how God's redeemed people should live in a culture structured to deny the lordship of Christ. This passage has come up again and again in this book because of its clear declaration that God sets apart his people for his own purposes. Once we were not a people; now we are God's people (2:10). And that changes everything. We live in this world as sojourners (2:11) who belong to another world. This is not our home. The world has its cultural institutions that make claims on our lives. These institutions in Peter's time had literal power to define and control people. The state was an imperial dictatorship with absolute authority over everyone. The economy was based on the labor of slaves. And the family structure was built around the solitary preferences of the husband and father. Peter's rallying cry is found in 2:16: "Live as people who are free, not using your freedom as a cover-up for evil, but living as servants of God." The apostle is calling believers to an audacious vision. The freedom of Christ liberates us from the worldly systems around us, and then calls us to engage actively with them for the sake of the gospel! This is no simple or easy thing. This epistle came as a letter read aloud to an assembled congregation. Those hearing this letter read to them had just come out of, or are anticipating, a government-endorsed persecution. Yet Peter calls them to honor the very government officials who will likely carry out their persecution (2:13–14). Many new Christians are slaves whose lives are determined by the whims and dealings of oppressive masters. Yet Peter calls them to a submission that might even on occasion include unjust physical punishment (2:18–20). And for the newly converted wives, he calls them to be "subject" to autocratic, unbelieving husbands, to seek to be humble and modest, and to do good even if they get nothing but grief for it. This is radical truth.

Why would Peter's hearers even bother to listen to these words as they were read aloud? How could Peter expect people to accept the hardship of serving God in such hostile conditions? Frankly, it doesn't seem worth it. Not for wives, not for slaves, not for anyone not named Caesar. But Peter knew that his call would encounter willing ears, because these were free people! Whatever they experienced of cultural and social oppression, they knew they had been ransomed from a much more profound and evil bondage. Christ had suffered for them, to redeem them to freedom (2:21, 24). And he had set the example for how free people live in an oppressive world. As we now know, truly free people live as servants of God. They have purpose for their humble posture. Their honorable conduct and good deeds will glorify God even if it doesn't impress those around them (2:12). Their good deeds will expose the ignorance of foolish people (2:15). Their character in unjust suffering will bring God great joy (2:20). Their chaste humility will attract lost souls (3:1). Their humble prayers will be fruitful (3:7). And, most significantly, they will live under the eternal protection of the Shepherd and Overseer of their souls (2:25).

THE RADICAL REDEMPTION OF MARRIAGE

With this big picture in view, Peter focuses on the implications of redemption for the marriage relationship.

> Likewise, wives, be subject to your own husbands, so that even if some do not obey the word, they may be won without a word by the conduct of their wives, when they see your respectful and pure conduct. Do not let your adorning be external—the braiding of hair and the putting on of gold jewelry, or the clothing you wear—but let your adorning be the hidden person of the heart with the imperishable beauty of a gentle and quiet spirit, which in God's sight is very precious. For this is how the holy women who hoped in God used to adorn themselves, by submitting to their own husbands, as Sarah obeyed Abraham, calling him lord. And you are her children, if you do good and do not fear anything that is frightening. Likewise, husbands, live with your wives in an understanding way, showing honor to the woman as the weaker vessel, since they are heirs with you of the grace of life, so that your prayers may not be hindered. (1 Peter 3:1–7)

Peter's vision for marriage is culturally radical, and not simply because it affirms distinctive roles for husbands and wives in a marriage. Rightly understood, his words overthrow two burdens that have oppressed women throughout the world over the centuries. His call to the women effectively frees them from being defined by the men who would dominate them. It is true that Peter is advocating a submissive posture of the wife to the husband. This is entirely consistent with the pattern for marriage expressed throughout Scripture. The difference is what determines that submission. In Peter's culture, submission was demanded by men and went beyond a willingness to support male headship. A married woman's body and soul belonged under the lordship of the husband. But Peter begins his instructions with a comparison: "Likewise, wives . . ." (3:1). Likewise to what? The end of chapter 2 makes it clear. In the way Jesus submitted himself for the sake of redemption (2:21–25), wives can willingly submit themselves to a redemptive role in marriage. The key is this: their submission is to Christ as Lord and not to any man as lord. Belonging to Christ means they will never submit to a man in anything that would dishonor their true Lord. Serving God's greater purpose for marriage in the roles God has defined is a radical reorientation for anyone in the trap of a troubled marriage.

In 3:3–4 Peter then undermines the other great oppressor of women—impossible and transient cultural standards of beauty that define femininity by outward appearance, as opposed to quality of heart and soul. And just to be inclusive, he issues a call to husbands to risk social disgrace by rejecting the prevailing oppressive model of masculinity in favor of gentle, understanding, and self-sacrificing leadership in the home. Much is made of what wives are called to in this passage, but there is also a reorientation from cultural manhood to true biblical masculinity in this passage that was radical in Peter's day and remains so today. What can all this mean for a troubled marriage? It means that those whom Jesus has set free are free indeed (John 8:36). We are never owned by our circumstances, by the failures of a spouse, or by the world in which we live. We are owned by our Redeemer (Titus 2:14) and defined by him. When we face a troubled marriage, we know that Jesus is working in our situation to bring true freedom that isn't bound by past failures, present problems, or future uncertainty. I've seen husbands and wives embrace this fundamental gospel theme and begin to see hope for themselves and their spouse, gain courage for addressing hard issues, and faith for the heart work that is always at the center of redeeming troubled marriages.

Friends, this is where we start to get out of the trap of a troubled marriage. If you are a redeemed sinner, you are not defined by your marriage, your failures, your spouse's weaknesses, or your despair and discouragement. None of these things determines what must be, what cannot change.

A free servant of God can take stock of the poor preparation leading up to the wedding. You can begin to see the deep-seated cravings and expectations that have controlled what each of you expected from each other in marriage. Now all that painful experience of how hard it is to live with another sinner can be put to use for the good of your marriage, rather than just rehearsed and rehashed in bitter acrimony.

A free servant of God can more clearly see the redeeming purposes of God in even the most difficult trials and failures in a marriage. Two free people reflecting together on the unexpected turns of life can develop and sustain a compassion for each other. You'll begin to realize that the trials and traumas you've faced as individuals are not just personal wounds. They are unique and important parts of your story. You may not have written it that way, but you can begin to see the divine Author and his intentions in crafting your story in the way he has. And free servants of God help create profound redemption stories out of even the hardest life turns.

A free servant of God will see marriage as a stewardship of God's gift, and will work faithfully for its daily good. This intense and complicated human experience we call marriage is at its deepest level a glorious display case for the love of Christ for his redeemed people. It is for us to enjoy with his blessing, but it is at the same time an invitation to the world around us to see redemption up close and personal (Ephesians 5:31–32).

If Michael and Tina can grasp this profound truth, it will revolutionize the way they think about their marriage. Right now it is a dead end, and they can't see a way out of the trap. But if they take their eyes off each other and look to Jesus the Redeemer, they will see that he not only has a way out, he has a better way forward. Rather than talking about their marriage as a problem with another person, they can begin to see it as a great calling that needs careful attention from both of them to see it fulfilled. It will be easier in this way to look within themselves for their own contributions and look beyond themselves for forgiveness and change.

THE VOW

In March 2008 the *Washington Post* ran a feature article entitled "The Vow"[2] about a married couple, Dave and Diana Kendall. About eight years prior, Diana had been diagnosed with Huntington's Disease. By the time the article was written, Diana was entirely incapacitated by the disease and Dave had devoted his life to caring for her basic human needs. It's a beautiful, heart-wrenching story of pain and loss, sadness and commitment. In the article it becomes very clear that both Dave and Diana had to radically alter their hopes and dreams for their marriage so it wouldn't engulf them in despair and defeat. The author, writing from a secular journalistic perspective, marvels at Dave's dedication and the tenderness of their marriage without quite understanding where it comes from.

The editor who oversaw the story was so affected by what he read that he felt he needed to write his own feelings. As you read his take below, think about the possibilities of your marriage, trapped in troubles as it is.

> When I encountered (the story) about Dave Kendall, whose wife, Diana, discovered she had an almost totally debilitating disease eight years ago, I reacted the same way most of you will: a stunned moment of awe at Dave's devotion and sacrifice, followed by some very uncomfortable questions. If I were in Dave's position, would I be able to react so selflessly, so honorably? Could I give up almost every single perk of marriage in return for an ever-increasing list of responsibilities? And the trickiest part: If I even attempted it, could I do so without falling into a swamp of bitterness and self-pity?

It doesn't take long to figure out that those are questions—like "How would I react in combat?"—that are unanswerable in the abstract. The answers must emerge, if, God forbid, you ever find yourself in that situation, in the day-after-day-after-day reality in which you learn things about yourself that only those under fire can know.[3]

You may be under fire in a troubled marriage. Or standing in the dark, not knowing where to go next. There is a way through, a way free people can walk in dependence and submission to the will of their Master. God promises that as you walk that way, he will give grace for change, light for the path, and mercy for stumbles along the way. And there will be people who see you emerge from the cave into the sunlight of hope who may come to know the Redeemer through your freedom story.

Chapter 10

FREE IN A WORLD OF TRAPS

O ur last visit is with William, the son of privilege who is trapped between two worlds. Unlike some of the other trapped people we've met, William isn't a composite character. He's a real-life person, though not from our time. His full name is William Legge, but he would have been more properly known in his day as William Legge, Viscount Lewisham, 2nd Earl of Dartmouth. He lived in England from 1731 to 1801, which places him in the middle of two significant historical events, the Evangelical Revival and the American Revolution. William would find himself caught between the two in a very personal way.

William, or Lord Dartmouth as he was known, had been born into high church nobility. But in his younger days he encountered the evangelical revival stoked by the preaching of John and Charles Wesley and George Whitefield. Through their ministry he was redeemed to an authentic faith in Christ, and from that point on his life was dedicated to the service of the King of kings. But by virtue of his standing as a noble and his skills and connections in politics, William ascended in the service of the King of England as well.

Sometime following his conversion, Lord Dartmouth became aware of the radical conversion of John Newton, the slave trader who would become a hymn writer and a leader in the opposition to the British slave trade. In 1764 Newton was seeking ordination into the Church of England, and Dartmouth agreed to be his sponsor. This led to the appointment of the former infidel to the parish pastorate at Olney, which was overseen by Dartmouth. A lifelong friendship developed between the pastor who had escaped the world and the politician who was rising to the top of it.

Fast-forward ten years. William Legge had risen to the position of Secretary of State for all of the English colonies, including the American colonies. It was 1774 and things weren't going well in William's job. Tea had been spilt in Boston Harbor and blood was beginning to boil throughout England's most prized colonial possession. As Secretary of State, Lord Dartmouth preferred a conciliatory posture toward the colonies, but this was becoming increasingly hard to maintain as the protest became a revolt. By 1775 he had authorized force to quell the rebellion but he also resigned his position because he didn't want to prosecute an all-out war against fellow Englishmen. Over the next year he continued to serve as a key advisor to the king as the situation in America unraveled.

Dartmouth was in political turmoil, but found himself in a spiritual bind as well. His soul was troubled by the moral compromises that seemed necessary in politics and by the immoral society in which he traveled. His burden was to find a way to live out the words we have been considering in 1 Peter, especially:

> Beloved, I urge you as sojourners and exiles to abstain from the passions of the flesh, which wage war against your soul. Keep your conduct among the Gentiles honorable, so that when they speak against you as evildoers, they may see your good deeds and glorify God on the day of visitation. Be subject for the Lord's sake to every human institution, whether it be to the emperor as supreme, or to governors as sent by him to punish those who do evil and to praise those who do good. For this is the will of God, that by doing good you should put to silence the ignorance of foolish people. Live as people who are free, not using your freedom as a cover-up for evil, but living as servants of God. (1 Peter 2:11–16)

William wrote to his friend and pastoral counselor John Newton for advice on how he could be a faithful Christian in a world that seemed so oppositional to his faith. The correspondence took place over several months.

One letter from Pastor Newton will be our focus. This letter was written in November 1776. Note the date. The British government was in an uproar over a one-page document that had been received from its colonies just a couple of months prior. The document included these provocative words:

> We hold these truths to be self-evident, that all men are created equal, that they are endowed by their Creator with certain unalienable rights, that among these are life, liberty, and the pursuit of happiness.

At the same time that William the aristocratic politician was pondering these words proclaiming liberty, he was wrestling with his conscience over the meaning of liberty as a Christian. What liberty did he have as a servant of God? Was he free to live in the full pomp and privilege of his station in life? Or was his freedom bound in some way by his duty as a Christian? We're going to spend this chapter looking over the shoulder of a man reading a letter. He is wrestling in his soul over how to be faithful to his Redeemer at a time when both worldly influence and worldly temptations are converging upon him in historic proportions.

WHAT IN THE WORLD IS THE PROBLEM?

Lord Dartmouth was confronting the temptation of worldliness. One commentary describes worldliness as "the enthronement of something other than God as the supreme object of man's interests and affections."[1] Another simply defines it as "the practical outworking of standards unrelated to the fact of God."[2] In other words, worldliness is a catch-all concept for behaviors, beliefs, values, and social structures that exist as if God doesn't.

The lure of worldliness is something every servant of Christ must face. It was an issue for God's holy people in the Old Testament. Though they had been set free from slavery in Egypt, the Israelites were constantly tempted to live like the peoples around them. They were attracted to the indulgences and customs of their pagan neighbors. They craved worldly political and economic success. Even when strong leaders and great prophets called them back to the worship of God, the draw to the world never abated. It was the great snare of the people of God in the Old Testament. In the New Testament this concern for the redeemed of Christ is no less urgent. To Jesus, the ways of the world are poison to a life of faith.

> Then Jesus told his disciples, "If anyone would come after me, let him deny himself and take up his cross and follow me. For whoever would save his life will lose it, but whoever loses his life for my sake will find it. For what will it profit a man if he gains the whole world and forfeits his soul? Or what shall a man give in return for his soul?" (Matthew 16:24–26)

The apostles made this a regular theme in their instruction to the early church. The pagan world around them was both enticing to the flesh and oppositional to the faith. It was a place of both tribulation (John 16:33) and temptation (James 4:4). The Christian is reminded that this world is passing away and can never be our true home. As we've seen, the people of God are to live as "sojourners and exiles" in this life as we move toward our eternal home (1 Peter 2:11). But while we're here, we're meant to make a difference. Christians are warned not to be stained by the world (James 1:27) even while they are being sent into it with the message of the gospel (John 17:17). Our necessary engagement with the world comes with temptations to be trapped by the very values we are intended to confront and overcome.

A crucial question for the early church, and for every Christian throughout history to this day, is something like this: How do God's free people live out their freedom in a world full of enticing and compromising traps? Often this is presented as a debate between liberty and license. In this debate, liberty usually means the freedom to enjoy the good things around us because we are free in Christ from the law. License usually means that we are taking liberties that true faithfulness to God doesn't allow. How far does our liberty in Christ allow us to go before we have given ourselves license to do what opposes the lordship of Christ? You can't just choose one over the other. It won't do to withdraw from the world into our own Christian ghetto, because we do have a responsibility to take the message of redemption into the world. And it won't do to live like the world lives, because we will lose the primary reason for which God has left us in the world in the first place.

When I'm wondering whether something I want to do is appropriate for me as a Christian, I'll often pull out this letter, written nearly 250 years ago. Why? I think some of the best advice for our current age comes from the wisdom of previous ages. None of our present-day temptations are really new, and it can be helpful to see how saints of days gone by dealt with their versions of our temptations. Also, our judgment can be clouded by the familiarity of the world around us. Listening to someone who lived in a different time and place can help us think of the principles beyond our own cultural confusion.

WISE WORDS TO WILLIAM AND TO US[3]

In his advice to Lord Dartmouth, John Newton begins by cutting to the heart of the issue. "When our love to the Lord is in lively exercise, and the rule of His Word is in our eye, we seldom make great mistakes."

In other words, how we relate to issues of liberty and license reflects the current state of our hearts toward God. If our prime desire is love for God and our prime directive comes from his Word, we will probably not err to any great extent in the use of liberty. Godly actions tend to flow from godly motives.

From this basic premise, Newton's advice gives us three good tests for determining how we live according to liberty. Let's call them the test of personal godliness, the test of missional impact, and the test of biblical wisdom.

THE TEST OF PERSONAL GODLINESS

Pastor Newton knew the wily ways of the human heart. He knew that the way we want to deal with the enticements of the world is by asking, "How near may we go to the utmost bounds of what is right without being wrong?" Newton identifies a common tendency of people upon a conversion experience to flee their worldly snares, only to drift back toward them because they equate maturity with an ability to pick and choose among indulgences. Rather than looking at what we want from the world and asking "How much can I get?" Newton exhorts us to another focus. True godliness calls us "to maintain communion with Him in our own souls and to glorify Him in the sight of men." In considering our souls, Newton challenges us to refrain from things that "deaden our hearts to divine things," and exhorts us to not "pursue, rest in, or allow" anything that gives us greater joy than our chief joy in God. In other words, let's live as if everything we do affects our fellowship with God and our witness about God to others.

Sometimes we can see how some liberties affect our fellowship with God, but we have a hard time seeing how they affect our witness to others. If I listen to death metal through my ear buds while I'm doing my devotions, I might have a tough time engaging with the Lord. But all anybody else would see at that moment is me reading my Bible. So my witness would be intact. Right?

If I have a beer at a ball game and somebody from my church sees me and thinks I'm a lush, my witness might be affected. But if I'm only having one beer and am not looking to get drunk, I'm good with God. Right?

Wrong on both counts. Newton reminds us that there is an inseparable link between what we do in private and what we do in public. If God is God, then he is the God of our private life and our public life. What we often call the sacred/secular distinction doesn't exist. When we live with a distinction between sacred and secular, "Christian liberty" can simply become the religious permission we assume to do worldly things. We can avoid an uncomfortable evaluation of our worldly pursuits by pointing to all our religious activities (quiet times, service, meeting attendance, good deeds, etc.) that earn us a right to a little fun in life. The problem is that we are never really in danger of too much religion and not enough fun. The danger runs the other way. This may mean moderation in all things, but it will also mean (as Peter tells us) that we "abstain from [things] which wage war against your soul" (1 Peter 2:11).

What is truly at risk is the sacrifice of true joy for false joys. Our souls weren't created with bipolar tendencies. They were created to find joy in God and him alone. This doesn't mean we have to go the way of the ascetics and reject everything in the world. It is lavish grace that allows us to experience true joy in God through secondary joys in the world around us. Christian liberty may be best understood as the kind permission of our Creator to enjoy the things he has created for us. I believe this can include things that we have created for enjoyment as well—art, music, sports, Mexican food, roller coasters, jokes, beach vacations, movies, Ford Mustangs . . . well, the list is getting a little long and a little too personalized, but you get my point. To rightly understand and enjoy liberty, we must remove the sacred/secular divide. All our secular enjoyments have sacred implications. And all our secondary joys must ultimately feed our primary joy in God.

THE TEST OF MISSIONAL VISION

After assessing the way our pursuit of liberty affects our own souls, Pastor Newton calls us to turn our attention to the way we live as Christians in relationship to others. In this he is applying the teaching of the apostle Paul, who advocated liberty constrained by the law of love (see Romans 14:14–21 and 1 Corinthians 8:9–13). Paul dismantles legalistic boundaries on what is clean and unclean for Christians and moves the issue to what will be most loving and beneficial toward those around us. Legalism does not give way to license, but to the higher call of love.

Newton advises us that, in considering our brothers, charity and prudence may require us to abstain from things that might be suitable for our liberty but would be a stumbling block for someone weaker. But to Newton, love doesn't just mean that we watch what we are doing around weaker people.

He reminds us that we don't always know who might be affected by what we do in the exercise of liberty. We will never know whose faith has been undermined by observing us when we didn't know we were being watched. Newton wants us to think clearly about what kind of example we want to be to others and to then live consistently with that conviction. "And it seems that an obligation to this sort of self-denial rises, and is strengthened, in proportion to the weight and influence of our characters." In other words, those who aspire to greater influence for God should be all the more concerned about their example to others.

The important thing here is that we are not motivated by what others think of us. That would be falling into the approval trap. We are, rather, motivated by a love for God and others that will seek to ensure that our lives are lived for the "mutual upbuilding" (as Paul says it in Romans 14:19) of our brothers and sisters in the faith. We don't simply think in terms of avoiding what might cause others to stumble. We want our lives to strengthen the faith of others as we make decisions regarding liberty. Liberty strained through the law of love will be liberty well expressed.

Pastor Newton then extends this principle to our mission to the lost. "There is a duty, and a charity likewise, which we owe to the world at large, as well as a faithfulness to God and His grace, in our necessary converse among them." In considering the unbeliever, we should desire that their interactions with us not only leave them conscious of our graciousness, but our set-apartness as well.

This is what Peter is referring to when he talks about "honorable conduct" (1 Peter 2:12). In holiness we live for the glory of God; in graciousness we live for the benefit of the lost. Our exercise of liberty should always have in view the saving purposes of God for the unbelieving world around us. What they know about us should not be explainable apart from the light of Christ within us (Matthew 5:14–16). This is a missional vision as relevant in our day as it was in Lord Dartmouth's. As Newton sums up, "Happy are they who are favored with most of the holy unction, and best enabled to manifest to all around them, by their spirit, tempers, and conversations, what are the proper design and genuine effect of His gospel upon the hearts of sinners."

THE TEST OF BIBLICAL WISDOM

Pastor Newton next takes a step back and looks at the unbelieving world as a system of doing life. Newton was, if anything, extraordinarily practical in his spiritual counsel. He'd spent years in the worldliest of world systems—the trading of human beings as property in the form of slavery. As a redeemed sinner now engaged in the care of souls, he understood firsthand both the enterprise and enticements of the world. He knew that withdrawal from the world was not an option for the believer. Here's his interesting solution.

> In our way of little life in the country, serious people often complain of the snares they meet with from worldly people, and yet they must mix with them to get a livelihood. I advise them, if they can, to do their business with the world as they do it in the rain. If their business calls them abroad, they will not leave it undone for fear of being a little wet; but then, when it is done, they

presently seek shelter and will not stand in the rain for pleasure. So providential and necessary calls of duty that lead us into the world will not hurt us, if we find the spirit of the world unpleasant and are glad to retire from it, and keep out of it as much as our relative duties will permit. That which is our cross is not so likely to be our snare; but if that spirit which we should always watch and pray against, infects and assimilates our minds to itself, then we are sure to suffer loss, and act below the dignity of our profession.

Most of us work in occupations that function entirely on systems created in the world. We may be an engineer, or a construction worker, or a health care professional, or a student. Unless we are engaged in vocational Christian ministry, we know that the world in which we work doesn't revolve around the glory and mission of God. So we must learn how to succeed in it without becoming a part of it. In Newton's analogy, there is no way to not get wet with the world. But there is no reason we have to live soaked with the world. We know that we're soaked with the world when its values, language, and choices become ours.

How wet with the world are you? Do you, like the street-smart city worker, have a skill at finding those dry shelter spots in the rain so that you can do your business without getting soaked? Or have you just gotten used to being soaking wet? One way we make sure that the wetness of the world doesn't become our preferred existence is to cultivate and protect our love for the things of God. The true joy of the Lord, the fellowship of the saints, and the untarnished satisfaction of servanthood are shelters from the rain of the world that we can always access—if we are looking for them. The Christian who exercises liberty well will know when she's getting wet with the world, and how to keep dry as well.

We're talking about a properly balanced life. And the balance between engagement with the world and withdrawal from it isn't the only balance that is in play. What about the balance between work and leisure? John Newton was acutely aware of the time he had wasted in life before submitting himself to the Savior. He had a deep desire to use his remaining time on earth in spiritual productivity. But he also recognized a certain folly in activity compulsively done, even religious activity. He understood that work in the world was taxing, and that simply bouncing from the intensity of everyday life into equally intense religious activities wasn't sustainable Christianity. He understood that leisure had its place, if for no other reason than to provide a pause in life from constant secular, or even religious, business.

Newton would appreciate the value of a walk in the woods, a good book, hanging out with friends, listening to music, a good meal and all that goes with it. But he also saw the snare of escaping into leisure with the same intensity that we pursue the rest of life. The modern slogan, "Work hard, play hard," wouldn't be his advice. A carefully balanced approach to activity and rest is crucial to healthy spirituality. Because, more than anything else, what we do in our leisure has the greatest possibility of wasting the precious time God has given us.

In our culture it is the couch potato, internet zombie, gaming geek, gym junkie, binge-watcher, hobby-obsessive time-waster that is the issue. We can't rationalize indulging in lavish leisure because we have just been doing intense work or intense ministry. Too much leisure takes over our time and our lives like weeds in a garden. Newton's solution to the balance problem in life is simple. In considering the preciousness of time, we should not be compelled to constant productivity, but should allow our rest to have its appropriate effect. Leisure is not retreat from spiritual productivity, but activity that refreshes us for renewed spiritual productivity.

Another issue requiring wisdom is the Christian's place in the culture. John Newton kept his finger on the pulse of his society. He was acutely aware of the winds of fashion and popularity, and the quirky human tendency to feel the need to be relevant to the world around us. What we want and enjoy is significantly determined by the culture we're immersed in. Our values are shaped by cultural values. Perhaps our great concern is not that we might throw ourselves into the worldliness trap in one great leap, but that we will be enveloped by it just enough so that it traps us a little bit at a time.

What was Newton's antidote to cultural captivation? In considering what is popular, we should have a "peculiar spirit," carefully discerning those present-day enticements that are particular expressions of the spirit of the age and not building our lifestyle around them. In talking about a peculiar spirit, Newton is drawing on the same redemptive covenant language we have been exploring throughout this book. So we read from the King James translation that Newton used, "For thou art an holy people unto the LORD thy God, and the LORD hath chosen thee to be a *peculiar* people unto himself, above all the nations that are upon the earth" (Deuteronomy 14:2, emphasis added).

To Newton, this peculiar spirit needs to be expressed in all our connections. If our family obligations require us to compromise our biblical convictions, then we may need to be considered peculiar by our families. If our role in the world invites conformity to its ways, we need to be peculiar there. This was very real to William Legge. He was a politician coming from a politically connected family. In his day, honoring the family and success in politics meant loyalty to a political party and what it stood for. To be a biblical Christian, however, meant that you couldn't simply go with the political status quo. That was Lord Dartmouth's dilemma. How could he be politically influential and biblically committed at the same time? How could he carry on the family name when his life had been bought by Christ? He was in the middle of the issue of what to do about the American Revolution. But eventually his biblical convictions would draw him into the unpopular position of opposing the slave trade. His stances on this issue would cost him considerably in terms of his reputation and his worldly influence. His family allegiance was questioned. To be peculiar was costly to William Legge. It will be costly to us as well.

John Newton's words are particularly relevant when we think about what it means to be missional. Christians need to live among and befriend those they seek to reach with the gospel. There is good reason in this—we do need to share truth with both our words and our lives. But the slippery slope approaches when we become so involved with our mission field that we forget the mission task. We get too like the people we're trying to reach. To be honest, I've done my share of "over-incarnating" over the years—sitting in on ungodly conversations, imbibing when I could have wisely abstained, telling stories that accent my raucous past rather than my pedestrian present. Logically, we want to be relevant to those we are trying to reach so we can build relationships. But Newton helps us to see that if we buy too much into the relevance logic, we may misrepresent the more significant evidence of God in our lives—our peculiarity. The world is full of people who are trying to be relevant. What it needs are people who are willing to be peculiar. The mark of an authentic work of God in a person will combine a discernible holiness of character with an attractive, gracious spirit.

FROM TRAPS TO FREEDOM

We live in a world full of traps. Let's remember that the freedom we possess was bought by the precious blood of Jesus. We have been redeemed from slavery to serve the interests of our Lord, and live in this world for his glory. To once again visit the language of Peter,

> [We] are a chosen race, a royal priesthood, a holy nation, a people for his own possession, that [we] may proclaim the excellencies of him who called [us] out of darkness into his marvelous light. Once [we] were not a people, but now [we] are God's people; once [we] had not received mercy, but now [we] have received mercy. . . . Live as people who are free . . . living as servants of God. (1 Peter 2:9–10, 16)

As we end this book, I hope your gratefulness for our Great Redeemer has been deepened and your vision to serve him has been stirred, even as you face the traps in your life. We have been ransomed for God, redeemed to serve our Lord Jesus Christ. There is no greater freedom!

Long my imprisoned spirit lay
Fast bound in sin and nature's night;
Thine eye diffused a quickening ray,
I woke, the dungeon flamed with light;
My chains fell off, my heart was free,
I rose, went forth, and followed thee.
My chains fell off, my heart was free,
I rose, went forth, and followed thee![4]

ENDNOTES

Introduction

1. Mark Sichel, "Trapped in America: You Do Have a Choice," *Psychology Today*, May 7, 2010, https://www.psychologytoday.com/blog/the-therapist-is-in/201005/trapped-in-america-you-do-have-choice.

2. Jerry Bridges, *The Gospel for Real Life* (Colorado Springs: NavPress, 2002), 12.

3. Ibid., 15.

Chapter 2: Not as Free as We Want to Be

1. Jon Clifton, "Americans Less Satisfied with Freedom," *Gallup*, July 1, 2014, http://www.gallup.com/poll/172019/americans-less-satisfied-freedom.aspx.

2. Rachael Dymski, "The Busy Trap," *Relevant Magazine*, March 26, 2013, http://www.relevantmagazine.com/life/whole-life/busy-trap#Hgi6SZD5vzo5LOeb.99.

3. John Hospers, "Free Will and Psychoanalysis," *Moral Philosophy: An Introduction*, Second Edition, Paul F. Fink, ed. (Encino: Dickenson Publishing Company, 1977), 318.

Chapter 3: The Big Trap and the Great Redemption

1. G. K. Beale and D. A. Carson, eds., *Commentary on the New Testament Use of the Old Testament* (Grand Rapids: Baker Academic, 2007), 203.

2. Robert A. Peterson, *Salvation Accomplished by the Son: The Work of Christ* (Wheaton: Crossway, 2002), 329.

3. Göran Larsson, *Bound for Freedom* (Grand Rapids: Baker Academic, 1999), 89.

4. Benjamin B. Warfield, *The Person and Work of Christ* (Phillipsburg: P&R Publishing, 1989), 347.

Chapter 4: Real Freedom

1. Samuel Bolton, *The True Bounds of Christian Freedom*, Kindle location 2691.

2. It is difficult to find the original source of this quote. In an interview published in the July 26, 1969 edition of *Rolling Stone* magazine, Morrison owned the statement as his own. See http://www.rollingstone.com/music/features/the-rolling-stone-interview-jim-morrison-19690726?page=7.

3. Adam Kokesh, *Freedom* (Self-published, 2015), 7.

4. Taken from several sources, quotes from *USA Today*, 3.21.00.

5. Murray Harris, *Slave of Christ* (Leicester: Apollos, 1999), 138.

6. Leon Morris, *The Atonement—Its Meaning and Significance* (Downers Grove: InterVarsity Press, 1983), 123.

7. John Flavel, "The Method of Grace in the Gospel Redemption," from *The Works of John Flavel*, Vol. II (Edinburgh: Banner of Truth Trust, 1997), 275.

Chapter 5: The Approval Trap

1. Edward T. Welch, *When People Are Big and God Is Small* (Phillipsburg: P&R Publishing, 1997), 95.

2. Murray Harris, *Slave of Christ* (Leicester: Apollos, 1999), 101.

3. George Whitefield, *The Works of George Whitefield, Vol. 4* (Google Books, 2012), 355.

4. Charles Bridges, *Commentary on Proverbs* (Carlisle: Banner of Truth Trust, 1998), 587.

Chapter 6: The Laziness Trap

1. Attributed to Sir Matthew Hale in *Day's Collacon: An Encyclopedia of Prose Quotations,* ed., Edward Parsons Day, published 1883 and available on Google Books, 497.

2. Mark Twain, as quoted by James Edward Caron in *Unsanctified Newspaper Reporter* (Columbia: The Curators of the University of Missouri, 2008), 287.

3. Tremper Longman III, *How to Read Proverbs* (Downers Grove: InterVarsity Press, 2002), 122.

4. Paul Maxwell, "The Complicated Life of Lazy Boys," *Desiring God*, March 24, 2015, http://www.desiringgod.org/articles/the-complicated-life-of-lazy-boys.

5. Robert Haldane, *Exposition of the Epistle to the Romans* (MacDill Air Force Base: MacDonald Publishing Co., 1958), 565.

6. John Stott, *Authentic Christianity* (Madison: InterVarsity Press, 1995), 253.

7. John Newton, *Letters of John Newton* (Edinburgh: The Banner of Truth Trust, 1990), 189.

8. John Bunyan, *Grace Abounding to the Chief of Sinners*, 7, http://www.chapellibrary.org/files/4813/7642/2821/bun-abounding.pdf.

Chapter 7: The Trap of Secret Escape

1. Gary Wilson, "Has Evolution Trained Our Brains to Gorge on Food and Sex?" http://www.yourbrainonporn.com/has-evolution-trained-our-brains-to-gorge-on-food-and-sex.

2. Elyse Fitzpatrick, *Love to Eat, Hate to Eat* (Eugene, OR: Harvest House Publishers, 1999), Kindle Location 552.

Chapter 8: The Addictions Trap

1. RockMusicTV, "Kurt Cobain Talks about His Heroin Use" YouTube video, 1:00. March 26, 2014, https://www.youtube.com/watch?v=Z0cQSFCSENI.

2. American Society of Addiction Medicine, "Definition of Addiction," http://www.asam.org/for-the-public/definition-of-addiction.

3. Edward T. Welch, *Addictions: A Banquet at the Grave* (Phillipsburg: P&R Publishers, 2001), 35.

4. Tom McClellan as quoted by Gabrielle Glaser in "The Irrationality of Alcoholics Anonymous" in *The Atlantic.com*. April 2015. Accessible at http://www.theatlantic.com/features/archive/2015/03/the-irrationality-of-alcoholics-anonymous/386255/.

5. Maia Szalavitz, "An Addict's Battle with Painkiller Addiction Reveals Outdated Rehab Tactics," *Time*, May 31, 2011, http://healthland.time.com/2011/05/31/an-addicts-battle-with-painkiller-addiction-reveals-outdated-rehab-tactics/.

6. William Hendriksen, *Exposition of the Pastoral Epistles*, New Testament Commentary (Grand Rapids: Baker Book House, 1978), 370.

7. Welch, *Addictions*, 217.

8. Maia Szalavitz with Joseph Volpicelli from *Recovery Options: The Complete Guide* (New York: John Wiley and Sons, 2000), 49.

9. John Stott, *The Message of 1 Timothy and Titus* (Downers Grove: InterVarsity Press, 1996), 195.

Chapter 9: Trapped in a Troubled Marriage

1. Timothy Keller, *The Meaning of Marriage* (New York: Dutton, 2011), 87, 89.

2. Liza Mundy, "The Vow," *Washington Post*, March 9, 2008. The article can be accessed at http://www.washingtonpost.com/wp-dyn/content/article/2008/03/04/AR2008030402498.html.

3. Tom Shroder, "Editor's Note," *Washington Post*, March 9, 2008, http://www.washingtonpost.com/wp-dyn/content/article/2008/03/04/AR2008030402499.html?sid=ST2008030603276.

Chapter 10: Free in a World of Traps

1. R. V. G. Tasker, "World" in *New Bible Dictionary* (3rd ed.) D. R. W. Wood & I. H. Marshall, eds. (Downers Grove: InterVarsity Press, 1996), 1249.

2. C. J. Hemer, "Worldly" in *The International Standard Bible Encyclopedia* (Grand Rapids: Wm. B. Eerdmans, 1986), 1116.

3. The entire text of this letter in the version I originally encountered is identified as "Letter XXX—Cases of Conscience," and can be read in *Letters of John Newton* (Edinburgh: The Banner of Truth Trust, 1990), 160–6.

4. "And Can It Be," fourth stanza, by Charles Wesley, as reproduced at https://www.hymnal.net/en/hymn/h/296.

Speaking the Truth in Love

Our **mission** is to change lives with Christ's changeless truth.

Our **vision** is for the entire church to speak God's truth in love.

Our **passion** is for advancing biblical counseling throughout the world.

BIBLICAL
COUNSELING
COALITION

www.biblicalcounselingcoalition.org

NEW GROWTH PRESS

Publishing Gospel-Driven Books to
Build the Body of Christ

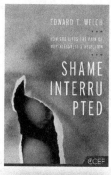

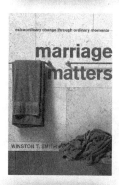
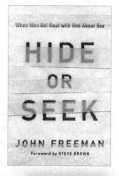

newgrowthpress.com